Time Travelers From Atlantis

THE COLLECTED ESSAYS OF

IDA M. KANNENBERG

Atlantis Phoenix
Missoula, Montana

Atlantis Phoenix

Missoula, Montana
AtlantisPhoenix.com

Order online at www.atlantisphoenix.com or email orders@atlantisphoenix.com. Quantity sales: Special discounts are available on quantity purchases by corporations, associations, and others. For details, contact the Sales Department at the address above.

Second Edition

Copyright © Krsanna Duran 2013

ISBN 978-0615934006 paperback

Cover design by Hartmut Jager

Other books by Ida M. Kannenberg

A SON OF OLD ATLANTIS

MY BROTHER IS A HAIRY MAN: THE SEARCH FOR BIGFOOT

PROJECT EARTH FROM THE ET PERSPECTIVE

UFO INITIATION: ULTRATERRESTRIAL TIME TRAVELERS

RECONCILIATION

THE ALIEN BOOK OF TRUTH: WHO AM I?
WHAT AM I DOING? WHY AM I HERE?

Contents

Foreword ~ Krsanna Duran.. i

Introduction ~ Krsanna Duran iii

    Continents Came in Cycles vi

    The Third Destruction of Atlantis viii

1. Atlantis and Lemuria ~ Hweig.......................................1

2. Time Travelers from Atlantis ~ Ida M. Kannenberg

    Summary and Hypothesis 5

    Atlantean Time Travelers, Contingent I.................. 10

    Lemurians, Contingent II 11

    New World Order, Contingent III 20

3. Mind: Its Function and Abilities ~ Hweig 27

    True Time, True Space 29

    Viewpoint of Manifestation 30

    Creative Forces from Viewpoint of Manifestation . 33

    Ghosts.. 37

    Telepathy.. 38

4. DevelopingTelepathic Abilities ~ Hweig...................... 39

5. The UFO Contactee Experience ~ Ida M. Kannenberg 45

    Night of the Flaming Moon.. 45

    Mental Telepathy.. 46

    What.. 49

Contents

How 54

Types of Manifestations............................. 55

Regression... 56

Remember When 59

Living with Hweig..................................... 61

UFO Sleuthing.. 65

6. Earth and Human Rejuvenation ~ Amorto 71

7. Life with My Live-in Time Traveler ~

Ida M. Kannenberg.................................... 75

8. The Great Contactee Hoax ~ Ida M. Kannenberg............. 87

Mind Travel 109

Myth and Mischief ~ Hweig...................... 117

Notes on the Contactee Hoax..................... 127

9. The Contactee Network ~ Hweig and Associates............. 132

Divided Pattern of Recall of Traumatic Event........ 142

Experiential Practice (Understanding and Pity)...... 145

Mind Power 145

Helping Someone Return from the

Psychic Outback....................................... 156

10. Why Are They Here! ~ Ida M. Kannenberg and

Hweig, Amorto and The Hidden One............... 162

11. The UFO Effect ~ Ida M. Kannenberg 165

Contents

Appendices

1. Author Profiles 175

2. Guardians, Creative Forces, the Source and
   the Radiance ~ Ida M. Kannenberg 176

3. Psychic Research Correspondence ~ Dr. Leo Sprinkle
   and Ida M. Kannenberg 179

4. Psychic Research~ Hweig and Jamie 181

    I.   Conducting Interviews in Psychic
       Research Outline 183

    II.   Events of UFO Contacts and Their
       Occupants Outline 193

    III. Analysis and Interpretation of
       Facts Researched in Parts I and II Outline ... 201

    IV. Summary and Revelations Outline 204
       Tracing the Coherent Pattern behind
       All UFO Manifestations 204

    V.   Analysis and Summary of Facts Ascertained
       in Parts I and II Outline 208

    VI. Interviews in Psychic Research
       Letters Outline 214
       Note on Hypnosis and Mind 214

5. Developing Telepathic Abilities Outline ~ Hweig 216

Biography

Foreword

KRSANNA DURAN

Atlantis was a fabled mirage for dreamers, philosophers and popular myth supported only by conjecture in 1968. Time travel floated in rarefied science fiction atmospheres in 1969, when Star Trek featured the slingshot effect in the "Tomorrow is Yesterday" episode. "The slingshot effect, also known as the light-speed breakaway factor, was a method of time travel through the use of an artificially-created time warp."[1] Star Trek fans embraced time travel as science fiction about future generations voyaging into deep space with Captain Kirk and the cast of the longest running television series in history.

"Not so," the time travelers said. Atlantis was their home 22,000 years ago, when they journeyed through time to the twentieth century. We are the time travelers' future, and Atlantis is our past, they explained.

Identifying herself as "a little old lady in tennis shoes," Kannenberg quietly and steadily recorded conversations with the time traveling UFO contactors, questioning and challenging them. Her voluminous notes and essays are replete with arguments, insights and speculation. She held her ground to find the roles a variety of communicators filled, their objectives and their limits: Extraterrestrials and spiritual teachers each focus on unique topics and methods within specific limits. Nature spirits, primal forces, and a variety of species fill unique roles in the panoply of visitors that UFO experiencers encounter.

The time travelers have a plan for the evolution of humankind through expansion of the species' mind. They are dedicated to thwarting mind control as we regain our inheritance of latent psychic abilities.

---

[1] *Memory Alpha* website. Downloaded 12-4-13: http://en.memory-alpha.org/wiki/Slingshot_effect

Seeds for growing the species mind were planted in thesis statements and outlines of four books in the 1970s. These contained
rudiments for developing the mind of the species. *Time Travelers
from Atlantis* includes theses and outlines for *The Mind: Its Function and Abilities*; *Development of Telepathic Abilities*; *Psychic Research*; and *Hypnosis*.

Ida Kannenberg patiently recorded one of the earliest and
longest UFO collaborations in the twentieth century, spanning
seventy years from 1940 to 2010. In those decades, the world
changed at warp speed. Atlantis and time travel became household words. Sunken pyramids discovered near Cuba's coast and
in the Atlantic evidenced an anciently lost civilization. Some
mind control projects – the infamously secret MK Ultra conducted after World War II, for example -- were declassified in the
1990s. Others remain classified.

Highly strange realities the time travelers spoke about at
the dawn of the Space Age came to pass. And we've only just
started expanding the species mind.

Introduction

KRSANNA DURAN

A lost and forgotten place of the ancients, Atlantis is little more than a fable or, perhaps, a distant memory for keepers of time and halls of records. A keeper of memory, the Greek philosopher Plato memorialized Atlantis at the opportune peak between the ancient and modern worlds. In his prime Plato had traveled in Egypt, Libya and Italy by 385 BCE, when ancient centers of learning and libraries were intact. Plato was schooled in history, religion, mathematics and philosophy. His accounts of Atlantis in *Timaeus* and *Critias*, written about 360 BCE, were the embers that kept ancient knowledge alive when the Dark Ages descended on Europe with Rome's collapse in the fifth century. In its quest for empire, Rome had gathered under its umbrella local indigenous cultures and dismantled them before collapsing. Europe was bereft of ancient knowledge seeded in older infrastructures, when the Greeks, Egyptians, Celts and others were marginalized with prosecution.

Well into the nineteenth century, Plato was the lone voice that had spoken for Atlantis, until Helena Blavatsky wrote *The Secret Doctrine* in 1888. She reported learning about Lemuria in *The Book of Dzyan*, written in Atlantis, and preserved in Tibet where she studied for three years in the 1860s. She was a scholar and initiate of the Tashilunpo lamasery in Tibet. She wrote about Atlantis and Mu (Lemuria) with great care to emphasize that the two civilizations were separate but successive in both time and space. Established when much of Africa was still beneath water, Mu was far older than Atlantis. As a witness of ancient archives, Helena Blavatsky's access in Tibet, India, and South America in the nineteenth century was unparalleled for Americans and Europeans. The Editorial Foreword to the 1927 edition of her book *The Voice of the Silence*, originally published in 1889, states the book was printed at the Panchen Lama's request, and that his staff and Chinese scholars had verified Blavatsky's translation of Tibetan words. It also mentions that Blavatsky had studied for several years at Tashilunpo and knew the Panchen Lama very well. The Fourteenth Dalai Lama wrote the foreword for the 1989 centenary edition of her book.

In the twentieth century, the Sleeping Prophet Edgar Cayce spoke about Atlantis and Lemuria while in deep trance states. Born in Kentucky (USA) in 1877, Cayce was eleven when Blavatsky published *The Secret Doctrine* while living in England. In contrast to Blavatsky's broad scholarly discourse about Atlantis interspersed in more than 1,000 pages, Cayce's information about Atlantis was revealed in readings that pertained to specific individuals for whom he did readings while in a trance state. Cayce's information is gleaned from brief passages relating to individuals in Atlantis in several hundred of the more than 14,000 individual readings he did. Although they spoke from different perspectives of Atlantis, both intellectually and historically, Cayce's readings expand on Blavatsky's expansive historical outline and, amazingly, do not contradict her broad view of the lost civilization in detail.

Rapid scientific advances in the late twentieth century substantiated much of Blavatsky's detail about the sunken continents where Atlantis and Mu were anciently located. Rigid conventions for defining continents did not exist and tectonic plates were a frontier for the next century when Blavatsky wrote that Atlantis and Mu in the nineteenth century. *Continent,* as a term, was translated from the Latin *terra continens* as *continuous land* in the sixteenth century. *Continental shelf* was first used in 1892, a year after Blavatsky's death.

Alfred Wegener's theory of continental drift, introduced in 1912, was initially dismissed. Geologists of the day believed the oceanic crust was too "firm" for the continents to "simply plough through." Wegener's theory was widely adopted fifty years later, in the 1960s, when magnetic anomalies in ocean floors were detected that could only be explained by the movement of landmasses.

New micro and supercontinents continued to be discovered well into the twenty-first century. *National Geographic* announced a newly found supercontinent in August 2011.

"'There are people who have put forth models of earlier super-continents. One, called Columbia, [may have] existed from 1.8 to 1.5 billion years [ago],' Loewy said.

Atlantis and Mu
90 Million Years Ago

Land was emerged on the Mid-Atlantic Ridge where Atlantis was on Baltica.

Mu was south of antipode of the Chicxulub asteroid that killed off the dinosaurs.

North America

Eurasia

Baltica

Africa

South America

Chicxulub

Madagascar

India

Kerguelen

Antarctica

Australia

Indian Ocean

Antipode

4

5

6

1

2

3

1. Africa submerged
2. Madagascar
3. Chicxulub, Yucatan

4. Indian Ocean
5. Modern Malaysia
6. Baltica Microcontinent

Atlantis and Mu were on ancient microcontinents 90 million years ago. Much of the African continent (1) was beneath water and India was parallel with Madgascar (2). Indonesia with Malaysia were not yet formed (5) when an asteroid impacted Chicxulub (3), and focused shattering force on the antipode (4), between Madagascar and Malaysia (5). The antipode was near Mu in the breakup region where the Indo-Australian tectonic plate fractured in 2012.

"And at 2.4 to 2.6 billion years ago, there seems to have been another major event," she said. "There appear to have been multiple cycles throughout time."[1]

In 2013, Brazilian and Japanese scientists announced another sunken continent 932 miles east of Brazil.[2] The scientists concluded the Rio Grande Elevation in the Atlantic is part of a submerged landmass because of the granite in its composition, which is the same rationale that L. Taylor Hansen used to conclude that large continents had been on the Mid-Atlantic Ridge millennia ago. The Atlantic area Hansen identified is the same region where scientists found the submerged remnant.

Continents Came in Cycles

Modern land formations originated from a handful of supercontinents that formed in succession, starting 2.1 billion years ago after a global scale collision. A virtual plethora of sunken continents and tectonic plates were discovered and mapped at the end of the twentieth century.

The Kerguelen plateau extending into the Antarctic was discovered to be a microcontinent in 1999. Kerguelen was above water three different times over a period of eighty million years "before it went underwater for a final time about twenty million years ago...Floor samples indicate that the land was covered by a coniferous forest. Unlike Hawaii, which resembles a chain of columns punctuating the ocean floor, the Kerguelen Plateau is a large igneous province encompassing a large amount of ocean-floor real estate. Today, most of the plateau lies 1 to 2.5 kilometers below the ocean surface. Two small portions, however, remain above the surface."[3] Southeast of Africa, the microcontinent is noted on the map.

The Baltic Shield from the ancient Baltica continent comprises much of Norway, Sweden, Iceland, and other parts of Scandinavia.

---

[1].Lovett, Richard A. "Texas and Antarctica Were Attached, Rocks Hint." *National Geographic.* August 2011.

[2] Reuters. "Submarine ridge off Brazil: piece of sole original continent?" May 7, 2013.

[3]. Lewis, Martin W.; Kären E. Wigen. 1997. *The Myth of Continents: a Critique of Metageography*

Shields are portions of continental crust that have not tectonical-
ly deformed, and are also called cratons. Baltica formed at the
same time as Gondwana, 514 million years ago, and derives its
name from the Baltic Sea.

An island that was above water in the Atlantic 12,000 years
ago, based on Soviet research that N. F. Zhirov presented in his
book *Atlantis,* is identical to Iceland's rock composition.

The Avalonia microcontinent is embedded in the crust of
Great Britain, Wales, Newfoundland, Canada, New England, and
the Atlantic floor. It had been connected to Gondwana and then
to Pangaea before it collided with Baltica and Laurentia in what is
now the North Atlantic. The latitudes where Avalonia materials
are embedded are south of Iceland and Scandinavia and north of
the Azores Islands. An Avalonia core that had remained intact
but embedded with Baltic Shield material after Avalonia's collision with Baltica is the most feasible candidate for a continent
where Poseidonis was the last emerged island of Atlantis in
11,564 BP.[4]   Traces of Avalonia materials are now part of the
Atlantic floor between New England and Great Britain.

Blavatsky's Mahatma anticipated these samplings of discoveries about continents and plate tectonics in the twentieth
century in an 1882 letter.

"In the Eocene Age—even in its "very first part—" [to 50 to 33
million years ago] the great cycle of the fourth Race [of] men, the
Atlanteans, had already reached its highest point, and the great
continent, the father of nearly all the present continents, showed
the first symptoms of sinking—a process that occupied it down to
11,446 years ago, when its last island, that, translating its vernacular name, we may call with propriety Poseidonis [Atlantis],
went down with a crash. By the bye, whoever wrote the review
of Donnelly's Atlantis is right: Lemuria can no more be confounded with the Atlantic Continent than Europe with America.
Both sunk and were drowned with their high civilizations and
"gods," yet between the two catastrophes a short period of about
700,000 years elapsed; "Lemuria" flourishing and ending her ca-

<hr>

[4] Mahatma Koot Hoomi's letter to A. O. Hume received July 10, 1882. Bark-
er, A. Trevor, Editor. 1926. *The Mahatma Letters to A.P. Sinnett.* Wheaton,
Illinois: Theosophical Publishing House.

reer just at about that trifling lapse of time before the early part of the Eocene Age, since its race was the third...why not bear in mind that, under the continents explored and fathomed by them, in the bowels of which they have found ere are the "Eocene Age" and forced it to deliver them its secrets, there may be, hidden deep in the fathomless, or rather unfathomed ocean beds, other, and far older continents whose stratums have never been geologically explored; and that they may someday upset entirely their present theories, thus illustrating the simplicity and sublimity of truth as connected with inductive "generalization" in opposition to their visionary conjectures. Why not admit—true, no one of them has ever thought of it—that our present continents have, like "Lemuria" and "Atlantis," been several times already submerged and had the time to reappear again, and bear their new groups of mankind and civilization; and that, at the first great geological upheaval, at the next cataclysm—in the series of periodical cataclysms that occur from the beginning to the end of every Round—our already autopsized continents will go down, and the Lemurias and Atlantises come up again. Think of the future geologists of the sixth and seventh races. Imagine them digging deep in the bowels of what was Ceylon and Simla, and finding implements of the Veddahs, or of the remote ancestor of the civilized Pahari—every object of the civilized portions of humanity that inhabited those regions having been pulverized to dust by the great masses of travelling glaciers during the next glacial period—"[5]

The Third Destruction of Atlantis

Atlantis was founded approximately 212,000 years ago (210,000 BCE) and underwent three separate destructions, according to Cayce.[6] The first major destruction was 50,722 BCE. The second destruction was between 28,000 and 22,000 BCE. The last destruction was circa 10,000 BCE, or 12,000 years ago according to Cayce. Helena Blavatsky's Tibetan teachers reported the last island of Atlantis sank nearly

---

[5]. Sinnett, A.P., compiled by Alfred Trevor Baker. 1923. *The Mahatma Letters to A.P. Sinnett from the Mahatmas M. and K.P.* Wheaton, IL: The Theosophical Publishing House.

[6] Little, Gregory and Lora and John Van Auken. 2008. *Edgar Cayce's Atlantis.* Virginia Beach, VA. A.R.E. Press.

11,600 years ago (9,564 BCE). Much of Atlantis' physical existence has been "pulverized to dust by the great masses of travelling glaciers." Atlantis' enduring influence is embedded in the
roots of languages and cultures along with traces in the geological
record.

Surprising mobility and a common mother language
among the people of Europe and Asia 15,000 years before present
(BP) explain shared information about abstract astronomical
theories between distant civilizations.[7,8,9] One could walk on
contiguous land from Gobekli Tepe to the gateway at the Strait
of Gibraltar where Plato described Atlantis before it catastrophi-
cally sank. The relatively small Cretan and Ionian Seas were the
only seas in the Mediterranean-Aegean basin, where ancient
Crete was landlocked. Turkey was a crossroads of the mother
language before the Aegean-Mediterranean basin filled with water circa 12,000 BP.[10]

The islands associated with the civilization of Atlantis
sprawled across the now-sunken microcontinents of Avalonia
and Baltica in the Atlantic. These extremely ancient microcontinents collided when modern continents were forming. They are
embedded in coastal areas of Scandinavia, Great Britain, Spain
and Morocco on the western side of the Atlantic. Fragments of

---

[7] Ghose, Tia. "Before Babel: Ancient Mother Tongue Reconstructed."
LifeScience. May 6, 2013.
www.livescience.com/29342-ancient-mother-tongue-reconstructed.html

[8] Pagel, Mark, etal. "Ultraconserved words point to deep language ancestry
across Eurasia." *Proceedings of the National Academy of Sciences of the United
States of America.* May 6, 2013.
www.pnas.org/content/early/2013/05/01/1218726110.full.pdf+html

[9] Wittke, James H., et al. "Evidence for deposition of 10 million tonnes of
impact spherules across four continents 12,800 years ago." Proceedings of
the National Academy of Sciences for the United States. Published online
before print May 20, 2013, doi:10.1073/pnas.1301760110 , PNAS May 20,
2013

[10]. Hansen, L. Taylor. 1969. *The Ancient Atlantic.* Amherst, WI: Amherst
Press.

Avalonia stretch across the Atlantic to the northeastern USA southward to the Gulf of Mexico.

Continental margins across the Atlantic, from the Gulf of Mexico to the Celtic Shelf off the coast of Spain, were wasted after the meteor impact at Chicxulub in the Yucatan sixty-five million years ago. The Strait of Gibraltar between Spain and Morocco is in the area of the Avalonia microcontinent. These areas had been subsiding for millions of year, before the glacial floods and in the present. A new subduction zone formed off Spain's coast in 2013 where the island kingdom of Atlantis once rose above the water. The single day when the relatively modern kingdom of Atlantis sank, according to Plato, was a day in the Great Year, or 12,000 solar years, known to the ancient Greeks.[11]

The larger civilization in which Atlantis was a kingdom included ancient Sumer in Mesopotamia and Egypt. Akkadian Ea of Mesopotamia dispatched seven divine sages to bring the arts and skills of civilization to humankind before the great floods, according to Chaldean historian Berossos.[12] Writing and mathematics fundamental for civilization building were undoubtedly among the divine sages' gifts. Collectively, the seven divine sages were known as "counselors" and are credited with building walled cities as well as possessing technical skills. Oannes (Uan), the Greek name for Ea's son Adapa, was the first of the divine sages before the great floods. Each sage was paired with a king,

---

[11] Planetary mechanics and locations of very ancient civilizations are covered in greater detail in Chapters Four and Five.

[12] Ea, also known as Enki (Sumerian. EN.KI(G) is a god in Sumerian mythology, later known as Ea in Akkadian and Babylonian mythology. He was originally patron god of the city of Eridu, but later the influence of his cult spread throughout Mesopotamia and to the Canaanites, Hittites, and Hurrians. He was the deity of crafts, mischief, water, seawater, lakewater (a, aba, ab), intelligence (gestú, literally "ear") and creation (Nudimmud: nu, likeness, dim mud, make beer). He was associated with the southern band of constellations called stars of Ea, but also with the constellation AŠ-IKU, the Field (Square of Pegasus). Beginning around the second millennium BCE, he was sometimes referred to in writing by the numeric ideogram for "40," occasionally referred to as his "sacred number." The planet Mercury, associated with Babylonian Nabu (the son of Marduk) was in Sumerian times, identified with Enki. (Wikipedia)

and was known by several names or epithets. They were depicted with attributes of fish or birds associated with the Underworld.

Anciently, the Underworld was a region comparable to Poseidon's seas and Zeus' sky. The dignified Hades ruled the Underworld with the powerful queen Persephone.[13] A change in Judaic doctrine in the seventh century BCE recast the Underworld as a place of agonizing suffering inhabited by frightful evil doers, which had not existed in earlier eras.[14] Before the flood, the sages were benevolent mentors who carried the gifts of civilization.

Devastating glacial flooding changed the world so dramatically that "before the floods" and "after the floods" were common temporal markers in ancient records, as if everybody knew about the great floods. A text, discovered at Uruk in the 1970s listing the antediluvian sages and kings that closely parallels the one in Book Two of *Babyloniaca,* affirms the reliability of that portion of Berossos' texts that survived through the hands of numerous scholars. Berossos was immersed in the Esagil temple culture as the center of science and learning, and was immersed in the cuneiform culture of his age.[15] He was born circa 330 BCE and his histories were written circa 390-378 BCE.

What was common knowledge in Berossos' age had changed radically 1,000 years later, when wars had destroyed ancient libraries of Babylon, Nineveh, and Alexandria. Rome captured ancient texts during conquests and holds an undetermined number in the Vatican's private archives, which it continues to keep private.

---

[13]. The Hebrews invented hell as a place of pain and suffering, which was later associated with the name Hades, but hell had no association with Hades in the Greeks.

[14] Assante, Julia and M.D. Larry Dossey. 2012. *The Last Frontier: Exploring the Afterlife and Transforming Our Fear of Death.* Novata, CA: New World Library

[15] Beaulieu, Paul-Alain. "Berossos on Late Babylonian History." *Special Issue of Oriental Studies.* 2006.

Ecological disasters that destroyed historical artifacts are among the problems of correlating Biblical dates with historical events. Moses wrote the first five books of the Old Testament while the Israelites wandered in the desert, approximately 2453 BCE (4453 BP) according to *The Reese Chronological Bible*.[16] Moses is generally considered the first contemporary Hebrew, in that he was the first to record the period in which he lived. Neither Moses nor any other living witness had direct experience of the history Moses formalized in the first five books of the Old Testament. Any historical possibility of the Great Deluge occurred long before Moses transmitted the account to the Israelites. The great floods could easily have happened in the ice age or in the period Plato ascribed to Atlantis. Dates extracted from the geological record could easily place Enoch and Abraham to the Atlantean era or ice age.

The Judeo-Christian timeline began the count of time with Adam and Eve's creation, as if the world had not existed before they did. Based on estimated lifespans of Adam and Eve's descendants, Judaic scholars estimated the world had been created sometime between 6,000 and 10,000 BP. This yielded a date in the range of 4,000 to 5,000 BP for the Great Deluge, based on Noah's birth. Nothing in the geological record supports huge floods 5,000 BP, although evidence of numerous localized floods exists. The geological record speaks for the Earth's physical history and gives perspective to the history that the Hebrews have borrowed from older cultures.

Glacial melt had started by 20,000 BP, and catastrophic flooding was abundantly evident 12,000 BP. The geological record yields dates between 13,000 and 11,000 BP for the most massive flooding. During intermittent warming and cooling periods at the end of the ice age, melt waters flowed to low-lying areas, then froze when temperatures cooled again. When temperatures warmed, water that had collected and frozen at low elevations would break loose and flood. Eerily beautiful coulees carved from bedrock in the American Northwest were created by ferocious flooding.[17] Waters that reached estimated speeds of sixty-five miles per hour stripped away the soil and cut into bedrock as

---

[16] Reese, Edward and Frank R. Klassen. 1977. *The Reese Chronological Bible.* Bloomington, MN: Bethany House Publishers

[17] Glacial Lake Missoula. HUGEfloods.com. http://www.hugefloods.com/LakeMissoula.html

they carried boulders from Montana to Washington State in North America. At Glen Roy in Scotland, glacial lakes that collected during warm periods and then froze cut perfectly level plateaus into mountainsides in three different phases.

Plato wrote about many deluges that had left only the wasted bones of small islands.

"Many great deluges have taken place during the nine thousand years, for that is the number of years which have elapsed since the time of which I am speaking; and during all of this time and through so many changes, there has never been any considerable accumulation of the soil coming down from the mountains, as in other places, but the earth has fallen away all round and sunk out of sight. The consequence is, that in comparison of what then was, there are remaining only the bones of the wasted body, as they may be called, as in the case of small islands, all the richer and softer parts of the soil having fallen away, and the mere skeleton of the land being left."[18]

A cosmic impact that scattered debris over four continents 12,800 BP left plenty of evidence on the ground along with escalated flooding after the impact.[19] Early Mayanists identified 12,500 BP for the date of a series of catastrophes that started with fire in the sky. After entering the atmosphere and traveling from northwest to southeast across Canada, the cosmic impact spread molten debris from California in the west to Central America in the south and Syria-Turkey in the east. It changed the ancient world and set in place the initial conditions of civilization, as we know it.[20]

Residue from the impact south of Turkey in Syria points to extreme conditions in the region when Gobekli Tepe was built. The Mediterranean-Aegean basin, which includes Turkey's mod-

---

[18]. Plato. *Critias.* 111b.

[19] Wittke, James H., et al. "Evidence for deposition of 10 million tonnes of impact spherules across four continents 12,800 years ago." Proceedings of the National Academy of Sciences for the United States. Published online before print May 20, 2013, doi:10.1073/pnas.1301760110 , PNAS May 20, 2013

[20] Ibid.

ern coast, was filling with water that formed the modern seas by 12,000 BP.

Gobekli Tepe's elevation on a high mountain ridge in Turkey was optimum for surviving floods, where flora and fauna might escape ravaging waters. Hunting and gathering were difficult with large losses of species and lowland food sources washed out. Life was precious at the dawn of the Holocene Age, when Stone Age people lived in the wild.

Like flapping butterfly wings, initial conditions 12,000 BP fluttered the forces that shaped modern civilization.[21] Geologist Robert Schoch, who studied erosion patterns on the Egyptian Sphinx and Gobekli Tepe, found they were constructed in the same period, circa 11,500 BP. He wrote about the Stone Age builders at Gobekli Tepe.

"This was supposedly the time of the brutish, nomadic, hunters and gatherers who, according to many academics, did not have the technology, governing institutions, or will to build structures such as those found at Göbekli Tepe. Clearly there is a disconnect between what conventional historians and archaeologists have been teaching all these years and the clear evidence on the ground."[22]

If anything could be more astounding than the intelligence and skill of Gobekli Tepe's builders, it is that they protected their intricate carvings before filling in the entire site 10,000 BP, as if to preserve them for posterity. More than the first temple in the world, as some archeologists describe Gobekli Tepe, it was a veritable library preserved in stone.

---

[21] Edward Lorenz discovered the butterfly effect in 1960 when attempting to predict weather. He found that even small differences in initial values for equations would result in very different patterns. Small differences in condition can result in widely diverging outcomes, popularly known as the *butterfly effect*. The flapping of a single butterfly's wing today produces a tiny change in the state of the atmosphere, for instance.

[22] . Schoch, Robert M. "The Mystery of Gobekli Tepe and Its Message To Us." *New Dawn Magazine*. September-October 2010. www.robertschoch.com/articles/schochgobeklitepenewdawnsept2010.pdf

The end of the Stone Age began with permanent settlements and agriculture within a 100-mile radius of Gobekli Tepe 10,000 years ago. The once-global mother tongue had been confounded. Historical records and monuments were destroyed in the ravages of success armies over millennia.

The time travelers had left Atlantis 22,000 years ago before the third and last destruction. Those who enabled them to escape the last days of Atlantis with time travel commissioned them, in turn, to assist modern humanity. They determined the twentieth century was most similar to Atlantis at the time they left, and in the late eighteenth century began preparing to re-enter our timeline to meet us in the present day. Many of the time travelers left Atlantis 22,000 years ago and re-entered our timeline in one lifetime, while we who remained on the ground lived numerous lives – happy lives, despairing ones and many shades between. The time travelers dismantled the last of their equipment around 2000 and blended into the weave of modern life on Earth.

CHAPTER ONE

Atlantis and Lemuria

HWEIG

Colonists from Lemuria had settled in and civilized that world you call Atlantis. Refugees from Lemuria came into Atlantis and aided in building up a fantastic technological empire. We had everything you have today, and much, much more, some of which we hope you never discover.

Your detailed account of all this can be filled in much later, right now we give only the bones as you have uncovered many of them for yourself. There are other bones yet to be found but you have the basics. We are not permitted to tell you everything one, two, three, as your own work develops you, handing it to you on a silver platter would not. Also, you accept the results of your own study with less skepticism than you would our handouts.

Suffice it to say, in Atlantis of about 22,000 years ago we already had space travel. Aided by advice from the same source that had rescued the Lemurians, we were able to construct and navigate our own ships.

The ruling class of Atlantis were all scientists (and were all psychic masters, incidentally) who also discovered and kept secret from the priestly caste (who were to a large extent separate from the ruling class and in violent opposition to each other) our discovery and utilization of a perfected TIME TRAVEL!

There were dissident factions among the rulers as well, but the contingent of which I am a member held strictly to the original ideals of communal sharing of all benefits and the acknowledgement of one God, the Primal Cause (involving that which you have called supra-consciousness, as well as other attributes). We gave thanks to Him by recognizing the Sun as the center of all psychic being (not spiritual); the priests turned this into direct sun worship, which we abhorred, and they began ugly rites thereto, and obscene practices. Eventually the rifts between the two factions, the scientists and the priests, became wider and more violent. When the priests, and what you would call soothsayers, foretold of the cataclysmic events to come our contingent of rulers and scientists decided secretly to "bug out" via time travel, utilizing some space travel as well.

We made extensive and lengthy tests and experiments to discover those persons willing and competent to undertake such a new type of adventure with us. Meanwhile we openly constructed gigantic "space stations" under the pretext of space experiments but we knew they would be our get-away vehicles through TIME.

The big question was where to emerge in time and space. Practicing our time travel experiments in the utmost secrecy we sent small craft into our future (which is your past as well as your present). We tried to make our appearances over Earth beneficial to whomever we found, and that is where the "Gods from outer space" idea came into your myths and legends. Ezekiel saw the wheel, yes indeed, a UFO from Atlantis of the period just before 22,000 BC, and not from outer space.

As we have told you on several occasions, we each live hundreds of years. We each had plenty of time for much experimenting.

We chose to re-emerge about 1800 CE, your time, for we believed the coming technological discoveries would soon bring

Earth to about the same stage of development as the civilization we had left. As simple as that!

There were many problems we had not anticipated and had to devise some very devious means and methods of making contact with Earth people and trying to gain acceptance by them.

Now we can go wherever we like in the smaller more maneuverable space/time craft supplied by Arcturus. Those who now occupy the planet, which we have named Tea Elsta, came originally from the area of Earth you now refer to as Lemuria.

They, themselves, had not yet progressed to the perfected building of space ships although they were working on it, but were aided in escaping a coming known catastrophe to their land by beings from another source, which we can never reveal, but who evacuated them from their threatened land.

We have contacts with Arcturus and they are now, with the help of sister planets, constructing more space/time craft and experimenting with new ones. We can go to many planets and places, but Earth is Home even though our continent and many small islands contingent thereto have long since vanished.

So you have put your information together correctly, Ida, when you theorize we came into your knowledge from two inter-connected sources, time craft from Atlantis and space craft from Arcturus. There is more than one space/time station.

The inhabitants of Arcturus have evolved differently through genetic experimentation and have mingled with other beings from other sources; they have no wish to return to Earth for any purpose except scientific study and experiment. We, the Atlanteans, do wish to return. You can, however, aid the Arcturians with some planetary problems.

We from Atlantis are very much like your selves. Some of those from Arcturus are quite different and, we have discovered, actually are scary to your people.

Now you can put all of your notes and comments and clues into a constructive order and come up with a very complete, logical, and we hope, acceptable explanation as to the origins of UFOs.[1]

---

[1] Dated July 3, 1997

CHAPTER TWO

Time Travelers from Atlantis

IDA M. KANNENBERG

Summary and Hypothesis

The manifestations we perceive as UFOs are only a small part of a total extremely complex phenomenon. The UFO people are the direct communicators, but outside, above, below, beyond, beside are tiers and hierarchies of other participants in the most complex and extravagant schemes to awaken Humankind to its true destiny, which it has so pathetically overlooked. They too take directions and instructions, generalized so they may use whatever specific means at hand that permit them to get an idea across.

The specific means then is neatly tailored by them and wrapped in whatever form and presentation the individual contactee is most likely to be able to take in and find assimilable. There is even room for the information as given, or the picture, to be incorrect, to contain errors. These errors are drawn from the contactee's understanding, and are re-expressed for the purpose of pointing them out, or having them pointed out by others in the future when their tale is told. A round about manner of correction rather than a face-to-face pedantic declaration, "You are wrong, this is correct."

In the mental telepathy events in which I have been engaged, I have never been corrected. I am always told I am right, "That is exact," and even that I am brilliant. This encourages me to go on looking for more brilliance and sooner or later bump my cranium against the truth that I was hasty in my conclusions, ill taken in my analysis, and ignorant in my assumption of facts. Then I make my own corrections as best I may and continue. I have not only learned, but developed. Had I been told I was an ignoramus I simply would have quit and gotten nowhere. There is only one subject on which they will blatantly correct someone, and even when he is right they may tell him he is wrong. The subject is TIME.

Everything that is done is done for one purpose, to make us THINK. The contradictions on TIME are for that purpose.

Think, think, think TIME. That is the message!

They cannot hand out facts, free and easy. Knowledge must be earned. Tidbits only are given out, bait, so one will struggle to find more. In the struggle is self-development. Thus we are made to earn any advancement, to suffer through the fires of "initiatory" experiences for any knowledge. What we earn is ours; we keep. What we do not earn we do not attain.

WHAT IS HAPPENING?

The Creative Forces are straining to extend themselves in all Nature and through us as well. When we collaborate with these Forces we allow them to extend themselves through us, and at the same time we ourselves are extended along with the collaboration, losing nothing of our individuated self-identity, but gaining new visions, new powers, and new realities. We become collaborators in the self-extension of the Forces of Creation. There are many other ways of saying this, but we shall stick to this one so as not to confuse any more than we have.

The UFOs try to make us see and understand all of this through their symbols and their telepathic messages.

We are ill prepared to understand and accept, and accepting to act.

This thrust forward in evolutionary time will not be a completed thing ever, always it has gone on, always it will go on and on beyond that. But right at this cosmic moment in our history, the Creative Forces are striving to push their own evolution forward THROUGH THE CONSCIOUSNESS OF MAN, through the mind of the Species. It can do so only singly and individually, but relative to the species.

The year 2000 looms ahead as though some kind of a turning point, it becomes much feared and talked about as though on the stroke of midnight December 31, 1999 the old Earth will suddenly shake itself and fall asunder and we who go to bed on that December eve will rise on New Year's Day as changed beings, or not arise at all.

Nonsense! The calendar is an arbitrary construction. It is not going to become a pivot of fate.

We will retire late on New Year's Eve and arise late on New Year's Day with more or less of a headache, just as we have always done, and the dear old world will go unheedingly rolling along on its course as it has and will for a long, long, long time.

If it should wobble about a bit on its axis it will adjust itself and we shall adjust ourselves to the planet's adjustment and none of this will happen on the stroke of midnight December 31, 1999. Such considerations as Earth wobbles must be taken up and studied by the latest marvels of science and preparations taken accordingly. We cannot resolve such problems either in terror stricken anticipation or find alleviation by use of the diviner's rod.

Let us get back to UFOs and their symbolic presentation of: "Your karma[1] is showing!"

The Day of Judgment is not about to arrive and will not arrive for it is always with us. What I did and said five minutes ago was "judged" at that very moment and already my reward and punishment are being meted and have been meted out, simply by the fact that I am more or less of a person by that act. As long as the effects of that act endure, so long will there be reward or punishment of that act grinding out. If the effects become cumulative and explosive, so too the karmic reaction.

It behooves us to guard our every word and act most carefully; naught goes scat free. This is observed in Absolute Justice and does not require any kind of a personalized God to administer it. God is, but is not sitting up there somewhere with a balance scale in his hand constantly weighing every act and every thought of every person on Earth

---

[1] Karma (Sanskrit) in Indian religions is the concept of "action" or "deed", understood as that which causes the entire cycle of cause and effect (i.e., the cycle called saṃsāra). Originating in ancient India, Karma is part of Hindu, Jain, Buddhist, and Sikh philosophies. (Wikipedia)

or elsewhere. He has better things to do. There are sunsets to watch and singing birds to listen to and flowers to train. Were He to watch so meticulously the activities of men as currently expressed, He would certainly become divinely ill!

Our problem is and has always been that while we can see the results of our acts of commission in our polluted air and employment difficulties and energy problems, we overlook entirely our "acts" of omission, our non-acts. It is hard to see what isn't there. Did we see them, we might resolve them. If we do not know they are there we cannot do anything about them, unless we somehow have them brought to our attention. Words of exhortation might do some good, but it is too difficult to reconcile the confused "Babel" of hundreds and hundreds of conflicting words. Something totally different is needed for this age of man.

It has been told me that no person yet has been able to tell the whole truth about their experiences aboard or seemingly aboard, a UFO; that always there are stops put on their memory and certain confusions or illusions put into their minds. When the time is ready these illusions and stops shall be lifted and the true and complete story of their experiences can then be told. Only then can the symbolic meaning be adequately interpreted and understood.

Perhaps when the time is ready an INTERPRETER will come.

Now back to nutz and boltz. And their emphasis on TIME.

The UFOs have an axe of their own to grind and would much prefer to approach us on a straightforward reveal-eveiything status. But they are only part of a much larger, complex, long conceived plan and must play their proper role therein, requiring the utmost patience and circumlocutions on their part, all of which they carry out with a great deal of camouflage.

The entire scheme must move forward in each of the experiences to the benefit of ah, though the UFO people must certainly chafe at the bit, for their personal problem is urgent and their time limited. Because of this urgency their methods are sometimes abrupt and scarifying.

When they know us so imperfectly and must utilize symbols to fit the hoped for understanding of each individual witness, they must be hard put to find proper means and methods for getting their meaning and purpose across. How much easier just to drop down on a sunny day and say, "Hi, neighbor!" But the larger scheme does not permit this.

They are somewhat as teachers, "To awaken and make aware," they said. And by their antics they try above all else to make us think, to wonder, compare notes, work together so we might be prepared for the larger collaboration that is to come, relative to our own consciousness expansion, as a whole, as a species.

To see through the eyes, or hear through the ears, or converse intimately with an Earth person as they have with me, and with many others, surely gives them the understanding of what experiences and what symbols they must use to "make sense" to their contactees.

Future experiences of contactees should be less rough but equally educational and the symbology of the experience should be easier to interpret. If this is not so, then my experience and those of others like me are practically for naught, or only for our own expansion of awareness when it comes to mean anything at all.

But individual expansion is not the nut to be cracked at this time; it is the consciousness of the species that is at stake. An evolutionary problem for the whole of mankind, not an individual, not a group, not a nation, not a race, but for the species Man.

The UFOs are saying in effect, simply, "For God's sake, "THINK!"

And indeed that is what they have us now doing, and have had us doing for many years.

Without doubt, the first thing they would like us to think about is our use of atomic energy and the hydrogen bomb and the necessity of peaceful collaboration on Earth, but this is only one part of the whole problem.

It does, however, touch upon their own individual axe to grind, their own immediate, and even more pressing problem, at least the problem of that particular faction that sits on a space island (or maybe several space islands) waiting a chance to come peacefully to a welcoming Earth before their support systems run out. This contingent is not prepared to go back from whence they came, and do not want to go elsewhere, though their various craft are capable of going _anywhere_. Earth is their HOME.

Atlantean Time Travelers, Contingent I

They came from the Earth and do not want to inhabit the moon or Mars or Jupiter or Arcturus. They want to come HOME.

For nearly two hundred years they have hovered cautiously and hopefully above Earth, waiting for some signal from their instructors that they might make a straightforward contact with Earth to tell their story, hoping to find acceptance.

And their origin on Earth?

Their mode of travel?

Their hopes and expectations?

This contingent is TIME TRAVELERS from Atlantis of nearly 22,000 years ago-[2].

The Atlanteans only want to come home peaceably and acceptably. Yet their larger task keeps them from declaring themselves openly. Until their part in that task is accomplished, the expansion of the species mind, they can be no more open than they are, for they too are struggling to attain that expansion. And I am sure there is great anguish among them that their contacts could not have been more knowledgably planned, and thus more profitably received.

Perhaps the experiences I and others like myself have gone through have been a training period for the people of the UFOs as well as us.

Therefore, I am glad I went through such experiences and am still somewhat under their tutelage and guidance, though in a more reserved way. I hope my constant squalling and bawling at their antics have shown them what not to do in approaching other Earth people. And I hope still more fervently that here and there I have been able to interpret for them what is a more acceptable way of approaching other contactees.

And now a question. If they have hovered up there going on two hundred years, how old are they individually? Their life

---

[2] Dated August 15, 1979

span is measured in our hundreds of years, six, seven, eight hundred and more. (What was the age of Methuselah?)

Next question: Did Atlantis have the technology to do this?

Witness: Edgar Cayce says yes[3], though he never thought of that particular question or of such use of his information, simply because no one ever had any reason to ask him. He could have found it.

But his case histories reveal the answer, obliquely, but in the affirmative.

Cayce is not the only one to touch on the reality of Atlantis and its super technological achievements, and the psychic masterminds, and its use of Nature Forces. These other sources shall be introduced and analyzed.

But was Atlantis a real place in a real time?

New evidence comes forth in the present.

The historical background of Atlantis and the supernormal aid received by its scientists and planners, this will be followed most carefully. UFOs seen throughout the ages will be accounted for, for with time travel the Atlanteans could appear anywhere, anytime and back again.

The Lemurians, Contingent II

The second contingent of UFOs, people who are not only aiding and abetting the Atlantis contingent and have themselves little interest in us except for scientific study, are those actually from another planet, but who originated on Earth, the so-called Lemurians[4].

The Creative Forces which now, right on cosmic schedule, seek to extend themselves through the superconsciousness of Man, were those who aided the Lemurians to escape through space travel from

---

[3] Edgar Cayce, Reading #440-5 Dec 20, 1933: "...And as we find, it was a period when there was much that has not even been thought of yet, in the present experience...."

[4] *Mysteries of Time and Space*, page 162. In the annotated copy of *The Allende Letters*, "Jessup made a brief reference to the same Iynkicidu cross.... Mr. B. explains: Cross is Atruscan (sic)-Lemurian...." Page 164. "Mr. B. clarifies the matter by stating: "Not a child, was another little man of Mu".

their destructing continent?, and later instigated the studies and discoveries of the Atlanteans to aid them in conquering Time travel, and in building their space islands.[5]

We, too, are now being impelled to certain discoveries and inventions which shortly shall make us capable of time travel as well as astounding space travels and a myriad other things for technological and scientific advancement on Earth.

If we just don't blow ourselves and our Atlantean cohorts all to hell and gone first, by misuse of atomic and other energies which we shall soon find.

Our sins of omission as a species are many and ugly indeed. But to awaken to that fact, to think about it, is the first step to meeting our species karma face to face and doing something about it.

We need to re-analyze our records of UFO contacts on this basis; many must work on this, not one or two. It is a collaborative effort that is needed, and when well-done we shall see where we need to re-construct our understanding and knowledge, and what to do about our problems, working from the topside down, that is, analyzing and reconstructing from the viewpoint of Cause, not effect.

This is the turning point, the apex of human mechanical achievement, we need not wait for the year 2000. It is with us NOW. We have climbed the hill of human endeavor laboriously and painfully. If we can adjust our vision to the viewpoint from the summit we can go more easily and blithely down the other side into the broad green valley of peace.

Another question: Why do the UFOs emerge at this exact time? Was it their own choice or was the timing chosen for them and they but follow the instructions of the instigators, the Creative Forces?

---

[5] From communications with Ida Kannenberg: the Space Islands "...were secretly Time Islands and the Atlanteans quickly traveled through time to arrive about two hundred years ago in our stratosphere. They have been seen and reported but the knowledge hidden." 2 September 2002.

Either way the reason would be the same. Because the Earth and Mankind at this moment are reaching the same level of technological know-how and karmic portrayal as those most advanced had in Atlantis so many years ago. They come back, not only to Earth as home, but into the same degree of civilization and mind awareness that they left all those ages ago.

It has taken Mankind 22,000 years to reproduce the knowledge, the awareness, the technological marvels that the Atlanteans knew in that far off age[6]. Not all Atlanteans, certainly, but the vanguard thereof, just as all men are not now entirely prepared for the evolutionary thrust into the superconscious awareness of the species self, of the relation of humanity to the Nature Universe, Universal Consciousness, or Humankind and the Creative Forces. There are so many ways of saying it.

If such times are similar now to the times they left, why do they not understand us better, and better know how to present themselves?

In the days of Atlantis all their activities and studies were on a group level. [7]They did not study nor grasp the individual and his individualistic relationships to each other. They existed individually as cells in a group-whole, and thought and understood and acted as a social unit or colony. Some men think this is the next step for men in the present, each to become a cellular part of a social whole. Heaven forbid! That is the basic philosophy that served to sink Atlantis!

It is instead for men of the coming age to act as individuals within a collaborative whole, but still as individuals reverberating to the individual stresses of single men in this world, not like some spiritless cell, unable to think or move without companion cells. It is through individuated being and spirit the Creative Forces can extend, not through a colony of ants each with two legs and a beard. Ants never

---

[6] Edgar Cayce, Reading #3004-1, May 15, 1943: "...New developments in air and water travel are no surprise to this entity, as these were beginning development in that period of escape." (There are many other references in the Readings to this fact that we are just now reaching the point of technology that the Atlanteans knew.)

[7] Edgar Cayce, Reading #877-26, May 23,1938: "...then such were not as household or as families like we have today, but rather as groups." (There are many references throughout as to group activity.)

evolved into anything more than ants because of their societal structure; in it they reached their dead end.

Certainly the philosophy of democracy was unheard of in the days of Atlantis, the individual retaining his stature in the collaborative, not collective, form of the whole.

And this is perhaps the main point of the species karma condition at the moment - a kind of spiritual democracy, collaborative, but not collective efforts, and the individual identity continued into the inconceivable future.

Collectivism may be fine for the deepest recesses of the sub-conscious, for that is where the findable past history of the species lies, in the collective unconscious. But for the super-conscious, collectivism is a horror to contemplate. The super-conscious is for the future and can exist and extend only in collaborative roles.

The UFO people do not understand us better or relate to us more gently and realistically for they do not understand the role individualism plays in our lives or the principles of democratic existence.

I am sure they are learning!

Theirs was a societal-group existence, composed of groups of priests, groups of rulers, groups of scholars, groups of scientists, groups of workers, etc., each group compartmentalized and paying heed to its own compartmental problems and duties only. If a person did not conform to the group standard or group norm, he was operated on by electrical or electro-magnetic forces, or hypnotism, or even knife surgery to be made to conform.^ There were no penal institutions but forcible altering of the mind that we would find horrible to contemplate in this day. NOT but what there are tentative steps in that direction. Mind altering is something not pleasant to think about in extended measure, for the question arises, "Who does the altering and why?"

Perhaps we need a full exposure of the Atlanteans most desperately, to show us what not to do and how to counteract some of that which has already begun.

If we have the books of Alexandria and all the others that have been destroyed or confiscated we would not be so perplexed, particularly as to who we are and why we are here. Our inheritance has been plundered beyond conscience!

But this is getting outside of our presentation here. We are trying to ascertain why those who originated from the Earth do not better understand those of Earth today.

We have not yet said the obvious: 22,000 years is one long time! People on Earth today have a considerable weight of history in their genes and cells, built in instinctual reactive abilities that the Atlanteans lack. They, on the other hand, are closer to the Creative Source of being. The same species are we but almost, one might say, at the opposite poles; they are almost as alien to us and we to them as true aliens from another universe would be.

I am not a mathematician, I am not a physicist, but I know there are obvious problems and I hope equally obvious answers here that I do not see. This is why I ask for a collaborative effort to study the UFO factor.

We need a great number of greatly trained minds and computers and only God knows what all to put it all together.

We need to distinguish between the major factions of UFOs (the minor factions are many) and to relate life in Old Atlantis, the technology and knowledge of that age, with the events we see disturbing us today. By comparing some of the things the Atlanteans are supposed to have been capable of then with some of the things the UFOs are supposed to be responsible for now, we find a lengthy and revealing list! And the binding thread is time travel.[1]

The two major factions are the one time Lemurians, now occupying a planet of their own, and the space island Atlanteans.

The Lemurians were in the infancy of space travel at the time they were rescued, 22,000 years ago. At least a contingent of them was rescued, for many went to Atlantis and other places on Earth to colonize and develop. Those who did the rescuing, the ones we now refer to as the Instigators of the present plan, the Creative Ones, are capable of creating whatever *they* might need by Mind Power. It was most simple for them to construct ships suitable for the Lemurians to traverse space to their new home planet.

After their settlement the Lemurians were given every aid of every kind, and instruction of every kind to build their own civilization, with all the accouterments thereof, mathematics, astronomy, calendrical knowledge, and every technology, even as the Atlanteans were similarly helped. The Atlanteans blew it. The Lemurians went on to ever-greater knowledge and skills, now having thousands of year's advancement over Earth development.

The Lemurians (we call them this to distinguish them, for we know not what else to call them), the Lemurians are actually not very much interested in the Earth they left 22,000 years ago for they have descended by generation, not advanced in a comparative few years by time travel. To the Lemurians Earth is almost a myth, a legend from out of their nearly forgotten past. They are aiding the Atlanteans now for several reasons, partly because they are scientifically curious as to their ancestral types and to see how we have developed 22,000 years later. They have planetary problems as well, and thus their own axe to grind in the overall scheme. Being more scientific than wise, they presently managed to create a little devastation on their "new" planet and need outside help in reconstructing a better life for themselves. We can help, but so can others, so they do not need us drastically except for one thing. They need human-Earth-type people to help them repopulate. The Atlanteans do not like their blasted planet, though some have gone there on temporary terms. Already the Lemurians have mixed with other types, human but different in form and nervous systems, to the extent they can no longer do so without losing all semblance of Earth humanity. They have gone as far as they care to in mixing "races" and they want some good old Earth bloodlines to re-establish the Earth-racial supremacy on their planet.

Not all of those we label "humanoid" come from Planet X. The Atlanteans brought with them many types of "workers" who inhabited the Earth in those golden days. The elves and dwarves of legends and fairy tales were "left over" Atlanteans, workers and so called inferiors, who escaped the final destruction of the land, as did many others, by fleeing to other areas, many of the "little people" going underground and appearing only occasionally to harass or delight their viewers as the case might be.

Altogether the present technology of the Lemurians surpasses that of the Atlanteans. Their spacecraft can fly rings around these of the Atlanteans. But their knowledge of science in fields other than mechanical applications has been lost, even as the Earth has lost the psychical and nature sciences. Therefore the Lemurians have as much to learn from the Atlanteans as vice versa, and as much to ask from Earth as to give.

All in all, it seems a time of mutual asking and mutual aid from all three of these related areas, Atlantean space islands, Lemurian planet, and Earth.

The necessity of constant change in life, the evolution thereof, is one of the basic factors in bringing all of this into focus at one time. Each of the three divergents has come to a single point in development of super-consciousness in the species mind, for all are of the same original species. All are at the moment of mind expansion or mind extension into the opening of the mind so that Creative Forces may become an active partner therein, a sublime collaboration, therefore one in which all of these factors can play an inter-active, inter- responsible part without any being taken over or controlled by any of the others. This evolution into collaboration far surpasses the instructive type aid that was given formerly.

Indeed a sublime collaboration and sublime moment in the history of Humankind wherever it might be found, on Atlantean space island circling Earth, on Earth itself, or on a planet colonized by escaping Lemurians, all finding themselves at once moving toward collaboration with the Creative Forces, hoping once again to work toward some measure of the purity and innocence of the species as it was in the beginning.

But to come to that point, which is still "some reach away," that is what the UFOs are trying to awaken us to, our proper destiny, and theirs as well, whether they be the people behind the nutz and boltz craft, on the space island, or behind the now usually illusionary craft directly from Tea Elsta in Arcturus (Planet X). Either source can use either type of craft and have done so on frequent occasion, but as they experiment they have each come to rely mainly on individual means as given. As the planetary ones have said, "Why send physical craft so far when an illusion will do just as well?" And these two separate sources are now collaborating and interchanging necessities so well it would be impossible to determine which of them is doing what.

So we have the Lemurians, many thousands of years in advance of us technologically and scientifically, and the Atlanteans only a little in advance but great psychic masters. We are trying to catch up to them by inspirational and other means directed by certain forces from the over-all plan.

Comes the moment of confession - for the UFO entities of all ranks in approaching us at first had small concern for us as individuals or even collectively. They were only doing what they had to do in the greater scheme of things to resolve their own problems. Following the generalized instructions of the Instigators, or Creative Forces, the UFO people tried to "Awaken us, make us aware" on their own terms, which we had no way of understanding and found harsh, even brutal at times. Our reactions thereto served to show them their tactics were not the best and slowly over the years they have been learning our languages, our ways, our status relative to scientific and technological experimentation, our plans, hopes, fears, desires, vicissitudes, frustrations, and all the rest of our complex societal and individual concerns. Gradually their approaches have changed, always trying to conform over more than a century and a half to the terms of our times and our understanding. Always we come closer and closer to the day of the breakthrough, when each can begin to know the other, to inter-relate on equal terms, and to inter-act for the benefit of all.

When they say they come to benefit mankind, they speak as much for themselves as for us. We have something to give them of equal value to anything they may give us of knowledge or science. Their acts and appearances are persistent and repetitious because they must make that contact of understanding and mutual agreement.

In the beginning they were greatly hampered by the lack of knowledge of our languages, but these were quickly learned. Among themselves they use mainly pictorial telepathy, pictures which show action and intent plus pictorial symbols rather than verbal symbols. This is another reason why symbology is more natural to them than using our speech.

Not only did they study the languages of the world, but the literatures and legends, beliefs and customs, and from all this information they derive the metaphors and symbols for their presentation.

Also through their communicators, those who have learned to interpret for them, they speak to many on Earth through verbal and mental telepathy, each according to his degree and method of understanding.

These mental contactees find it most difficult to convince anyone of what they have received; indeed they are fortunate if they don't get locked up. Or their information is buried in official or semi-official files, in papers which only a minority ever see, or buried in drawers, boxes and wastebaskets.

If all these keepers of the files could glance through this welter of material and compare it with the outline I make here, and bring all of their resolutions into public awareness, there would be an explosion of understanding.

Since their arrival in our times, the Atlanteans (and the Lemurians also) have been aided by these Creative Sources to advance their knowledge, and to manipulate time and energy in many additional ways to exhibit marvels for us. They have also been helped to establish subsidiary bases on other planetary members, mainly underground, where the smaller craft can reconnoiter, re-group, and replenish themselves, for the Lemurian planet is far, far from our planetary system.

I have spoken thus far only of the material and mechanical knowledge. We must also examine the psychic Mastership of those Atlanteans ensconced on their space island, or stations as the case may be, for they were and are indeed Masters of the Science of Psychic Phenomena. The "parapsychology" of 22,000 years ago was an accomplished and perfected science beyond all our conception in the present.

Mastership had never been an accomplishment of the Lemurians for their purpose on Earth was different. But since the advent of the space island they have been given psychic knowledge in exchange for their technological knowledge and aid, thus bringing them into great adeptness in the psychic arts, and they can now utilize these abilities almost as well as the Atlanteans.

There is a tremendous amount of material being printed every day in books, magazines, newspapers concerning psychic phenomena in general, indicating a great public demand for more knowledge. I cannot begin to list such publications and certainly cannot dip and skim into more than a few, for this would be a lifetime project. But I have read mightily and swiftly trying to catch the over-all direction and fervor and sentiment, and I believe the time has come for an exhaustive search, collaborative and purposeful, to find the reason for such phenomena appearing in such volume at such an hour as this.

Where did the Atlanteans get their knowledge, originally? We must remember their psychic powers were given them originally, in the beginnings; they had not yet been usurped from them or forbidden to them. Their psychic powers were greater and purer than any other race at any time on Earth.

Through these powers they reached other realms of being, other areas of thought and understanding.

Through these powers they received a contact from the Nature Forces of Earth itself, just as the people of Findhorn Garden have reached a contact on much lesser scale in this period.

Through the UFO people the Creative Forces from other realms can speak to us now.

The UFO people are the communicators only in this part of their contact, something they have been telling me repeatedly from the beginning, but I could not disentangle this aspect of their presence from the other aspect of their own purposes and intent.

New World Order, Contingent III

Now we come to Contingent III: those who are trying by fear tactics to scare the world into one unified whole, a world colony all neatly wrapped together and moving into unison which they shall then take over and control. How much easier to take control of one unified system, than millions and millions of diversified beings.

The Atlanteans of Contingent I have learned the inadvisability of group control and are striving to advance the individual identity, the separate You and I, but in collaborative efforts, not unified oneness, not collectivity.

Contingent III is working on every level of our thought and being to arouse us to terms of the unified whole, ideas of a return to God in Oneness in which the individuality is again lost in the All, speaking of the Spirit of Oneness of the Universe, and so on. These thoughts may have some excellence as they were in the beginning, but are now being used in propaganda for ulterior purposes.

Witness the beginning idea of the craft and artisan guilds in Europe centuries ago, and the monsters of the labor unions of today. The individual worker is totally lost in the unitary whole.

Contingent I, the Atlanteans, are presently trying to make us think in every manner of our individuality, not to make the same errors of group control they did. In this they are being trained, instructed, and inspired by the Instigators whom I cannot closer define than some part of the Creative Forces.

We, our very minds, are the battlefields on which these opposing ideas of collectivism vs. collaborative efforts are engaging in verbal combat.

I, for one, do not wish to be lost in a smudge of humanity. God gave me a freed will and individuated spirit, answerable to Him, and I intend to keep it that way.

World collaboration, by all means, but variety within uniformity, like a poem.

And who is Contingent III?

Those using the UFO manifestations for their own purposes though they have not one spacecraft or timecraft of their own are, in short, Earth bound entities, human beings, men, capable already of many forms of mind control.

In 1968, during my first episode with the communicators, though I had then no idea who they represented, I was told, "Even now there are twelve men secretly meeting in Egypt plotting to control the world."

That is all I can remember, and it is not a healthy study. I do not intend to push it at present, except to state: There is a renegade element of "other-borns" (but human) working with them, who can use every kind of psychic power. These are responsible for the least desirable manifestations which have occurred relative to the coming of the UFOs, for telepathic contacts that terrorize rather than instruct, for tragic events as an aftermath of UFO contacts, for animal mutila- tions[8], etc.

The Earth must not collect together in one terrified unit, but must collaborate with many self-viable parts in a collabora- tive effort. Like an octopus, if one tentacle is shorn, seven others are ready for action. There can be no threat of "divide and con- quer" if each part is a whole in itself, self-motivated, self- controlled, self-responsible.

Things Left Undone

We, as a species, Humankind, are being made aware of meeting our karma face to face. Not individual karma, not group or national karma, not racial karma, but species karma. And not karma due to those things we have done, those we face every day in our economic distresses: pollution problems, racial turmoil, and political strife. But karma we face here and now, focused by the advent of the UFOs; the species karma of things we have left undone.

It is not approaching Judgment Day. Every day we live is a day of judgment. Every act we do, every thought we think re- ceives, in the simultaneity of the act, its own reward and pun- ishment in full and equal measure. With each act effects are set in motion for which we pay as long as any effect lasts, even into future lifetimes.

In the species act of commission we receive our karma in- stantaneously. If we pollute our rivers we drink dirty water. That is not so difficult to understand.

Now we are called to account for those species acts of omission, or better put, for our non-acts.

These are as hidden to us as are the ways and purposes and understandings of the UFOs. But species karma of things left

---

[8] *Lost Continents*, L. Sprague de Camp, Page 65. Quoting Scott Elliot: "Atlan- teans ate vegetables, bread, milk, meat and fish. They showed peculiar taste with regard to these last two items, preferring their fish rotten and what are to us the less palatable organs for meat. They also drank blood...." (The higher classes however ate no meat at all.)

undone is the Great Key to UFOs and other current and allied phenomena.

It is the mechanics that are so tedious to find and symbolize. Perhaps in the word symbolize is the lesser key.

Symbols. Symbolic. Allegory. Metaphor.

The UFOs themselves are actual, even the psychically manifested ones are actual, they are not symbols, but the things they show us, the events they put us through, are symbolic pictures which we are meant to observe and analyze and understand.

We discuss here that smaller portion of the total karmic phenomenon which becomes apparent to us as UFO events and UFO activities.

There are two basic and quite separate manifestations of UFOs: those that appear visually, either in reality or hypnotically, and those that give no outer appearance but reveal themselves through mental telepathy. Unfortunately, exposition of these latter have been discarded, buried, burned, or otherwise destroyed with the label 'Useless" and "Senseless", and a big question mark raised as to the cerebral functions of the recipient.

The first type of manifestation, those which can be apparent to human sense apparatus, can be of three kinds:

Nutz and boltz craft, actual hardware, with or without corporeal occupants.

Semi-material craft, called up through Mind Power for the length of time needed. They are semi-reality, not imaginary or illusions. They cannot, however, be penetrated or acted upon or destructed by matter or material being; they cannot be touched nor shot down. As soon as no longer wanted they are dispersed back into the undifferentiated pre-substance from which they were called forth. Their occupants are psychic manifestations, equally semi-corporeal. [9] They look alto-

---

[9] Brad Steiger, *Mysteries of Space and Time,* page 206. Brad's friend told him about a strange caller. He ignored my proffered hand of greeting. In fact, I tried pushing his hand, but he refused to touch me." Again, on Page 207, Steve Yankee, describing the sudden disappearance of two men in black, "...About ten feet from the door I experienced an odd feeling - a sense of dissipated energy...." (It is possible both of these were semi-corporeals.)

gether like normal beings, however try to shake hands with one or step on his toe and you move right through him. A bullet would pass through him without harm, and he could equally pass through something as material as a wall or door without ruffling his hair.

Purely illusionary craft and/or occupants due to the hypnosis of the observer.

The purpose specifically given into the jurisdiction of the UFO people is to make us realize our species omissions, the things we have left undone, through symbolic representations of:

Things we should know and don't know.

Things we should do and don't do.

Living creatures and personalities whose lives and rights we should recognize and do not.

Concern we should show and do not.

Understanding we should have and do not have.

Recognition and thanksgiving in which we should participate and don't.

We are not given words of exhortation and revelation. The world already has myriad upon myriads of exhortations of religions and pseudo-religions, and cults and self-made messiahs, all of whose words and actions serve mainly to cut each other down.

Already there are too many religions and cults have become an abomination.

We are simply having called to our attention the hidden side of existence which can, in our present state of non-awareness, be given to us only symbolically or metaphorically.

Perhaps they do not altogether realize how badly we need an INTERPRETER to tell us what the totality of their symbols is meant to indicate. Or perhaps we are being given "the message" in so many different and sometimes seemingly opposed symbols in the bitter hope some of them will "catch on". Each recipient receives according to his possible mode of understanding.

The advent and activities of the UFOs also represent an initiatory process through which the human species is being helped to develop toward his rightful inheritance as participator in the activities of the Creative Forces[10].

By symbolism we are shown our omissions relative to the Nature Forces of the Earth and through ritual acts, often encompassing great distress and agony, we are initiated into the path toward collaboration with the Creative Forces.

We can, of course, fail again, either singly or all together, or we can push our understanding to its limits and strive to see and know the way we must progress. It is not through words of exhortation or by divine revelation the UFOs speak, but through symbolic representation of ideas that will direct and preserve our future.

What I write here is the result of many, many hours and days and months and years of study and anguish, and experiences I would not want to, could not, go through again.

Yet, for every YEA there is a NAY.

Or is it only that the total Reality is so vast, that no matter what we decide, we have to be at least partly right?[1]?

---

[10] From communications with Ida Kannenberg: "All the unnamed beings and the Creative Forces are always the Creative Ones as they are beings like the Elohim of the Bible." 02, September 2002

CHAPTER THREE

Mind: Its Function and Abilities

HWEIG

Mind is a different thing altogether from brain function. Mind is a "thing in itself" and lies over the mechanism of the brain in a complex array of patterns and images. It is, in essence, an energized field on which thoughts and concepts play in ever changing designs. The "field" itself is composed of minute particles, not quite physical substance, but not wholly energy, a substance that is found nowhere else in nature. It is not physical enough to be detected by any usual means, but not enough pure energy to be detected by the usual means of detecting energies. Lying in nature half-way between the two, there is only one way of discovering its reality other than by simply using it.

Alpha rays, beta rays, all the rest are results of brain activity.

Mind is not brain activity, though brain functions feed the mind with vibrations accrued from stimuli in the physical world.

The only means of observing the mind stuff is through use of the hologram. It can be so projected as a visible field of constantly actively changing patterns, and the patterns can be tabulated and translated, or in other words, this is visible mind reading.

The holographic projector is similar to that used to project pictures of physical objects with one more feature added which holographic projectors at present lack.

By utilizing the additional energy of the laser beam as a high energy compactor, the visual process accrues. Let your world figure that out. All the clues are here!

All right, we will hold up on this until you are more knowledgeable on holograms and holographic projectors. I simply cannot fight your skepticism every inch!

Rest a little.[1]

---

[1] In this remarkable conversation on June 1, 1979, Ida's mentor, Hweig, began a discussion about holograms, mind, and brain. When Ida protested she did not know anything about holograms and projectors, Hweig took a different tack.

Diaries about mind and brain, time and space, and reality and experience, which Ida wrote in 1977–78 were at the cutting edge of research in consciousness and quantum mechanics in 2010. In the three decades after Hweig and Ida had discussed the mind, brain, and holograms, science was catching up with the little old lady in tennis shoes, as Ida likened herself. Apollo 14 astronaut Edgar Mitchell wrote about the pivotal importance of the quantum hologram in "Nature's Mind: The Quantum Hologram."

The missing concepts that prevented the earliest investigators of consciousness from succeeding in their quest were 1) a generalized theory of information, and 2) quantum science itself, with the associated phenomena of nonlocality, the zero point energy fields and the quantum hologram. These associated phenomena are still not well understood but are sufficiently validated today by both theory and experiment to provide a basis for postulating a necessary condition for the existence of consciousness phenomena, as experienced in the observable four dimensional space/time universe... Theory and experimental evidence concerning the quantum hologram has been developed by Schempp (1992, 1993) and Marcer (1996, 1997, 1998), separately and jointly, based upon a new understanding of quantum mechanics...

The information carried by a quantum hologram encodes the complete event history of the object with respect to its three dimensional environment. It evolves over time to provide an encoded non-local record of the "experience" of the object in the four dimensional space/time of the object as to its journey in space/time and the quantum states visited. The question of the brain's ability, as a massively parallel quantum processor, to decode this information is addressed by Marcer and Schempp in "Model of the Neuron

True Time, True Space

The people of the Earth have considered mechanistic time, the sequence of events, to be Real time, and a relationship of separated objects to indicate Real space. This is NOT True time and True space which must be first understood in order to make observations such as those you call psychic manifestations understandable. Many other events and problems may be understood as well from what we reveal here, but at this moment we shall deal with "psychic / spiritual" manifestations only.

Mechanistic time we shall ignore for the present. The ticking of clocks, the sequences of events do not enter into this discussion. Multi-dimensional or True space depicts NOT a relationship of objects but the field of action of creative forces.

If these cannot extend within True space as it spreads out for them, then a convolution in space occurs as the creative forces are thwarted.

True time is individual consciousness. Taken as a whole it could equally be called MIND, but would include supra-consciousness, or God's experiential consciousness of self. The individual mind can indeed tap supra-consciousness when fully and perfectly developed. This is not a frequent occurrence. So for this work we shall speak of the developing mind simply as individual consciousness which is synonymous with True time.

In our delineation of the realities of psychic manifestations or "events" we shall leave out any concept of time in any form and refer only to individual consciousness. Awareness is not a complete enough term, for the consciousness we are considering here includes the individual subconscious, the so-called unconscious, and supraconscious as well as the conscious consciousness.

True time is individual consciousness, multi-leveled. A simple enough definition to hold in mind.

Working by Quantum Holography" (1997) and "The Brain as a Conscious System" (1998). They argue that an organism's ability to perceive objects as they are and where they actually are in three dimensional reality requires the phase conjugate relationship provided by quantum holography.

We are not reaching for exactitude comparable to mathematical formulae here, but for subjective interpretations through word symbolism that appeals to the non-scientifically disciplined mind as well as those more austerely disciplined.

The second consideration to explore is the comparable one of mechanistic space, as it is apparent in separated objects standing at some distance from each other, the reach from the earth to the stars, for example. This is a purely mechanistic concept and has nothing to do with TRUE SPACE.

Viewpoint of Manifestation

First, the world of psychic being is co-existent to the physical world, as we have often mentioned. It is another unseen component thereof. You asked, Ida, if space was not somehow convoluted and contains various kinds of reality. That made us reconsider our intended description. It is indeed convoluted as well as containing various kinds of reality intermeshed with each other. We had meant to stress the kinds only, but your sudden insight into the convolution of space frees your current notions of space, and our intended revelations suddenly become what you have sometimes accused us of, superficial.

Since you have come into the realization of space as not only containing a mesh of several realities, but also being convoluted, an excellent descriptive word, we can now proceed to give a more full and realistic interpretation of True space and all of your world's relationships thereto. This is a very important discussion right at this particular time.

We shall call consciousness True time, for it is true as far as your own mind is concerned. There are other dimensions of time, even a NON-time and another dimension where time and space are, well, not quite one, but interchangeable. Let us not get involved in these asides now, or it will become all too confusing.

Verbal expressions of your thoughts are quite adequate to the need in hand. Do not be distressed that you cannot express your ideas mathematically. Mathematics is only another language, an objective language.

Once you declared the objective of physical observation was only half the picture, the other half lay submerged awaiting subjective interpretations, or words to that effect. Quite so, and for now the symbolism of carefully chosen words are altogether adequate to express these subjective realities. That is, they are subjective to you from our ordinary viewpoint.

So if Time and Consciousness are one, and Space is convoluted as well as composed of several kinds of reality, we come to a very convenient understanding of both.

Remember Consciousness is True time, not NON-time. We will expand the idea of NON-time in our future writings.

For now we can describe the intermeshed kinds of True space and how they are enfolded in convolutions. Yes, it does sound "pretty mixed up," but patience. We will reveal it in order.

It is through the convolutions of the realities of space that some of the most mysterious phenomena have been able to occur. Such things as *time tunnels* and *windows in space*, as other writers have discussed, are looking in the right direction, but have not yet arrived at the fact.

The convolutions of space makes the strangest bedfellows, for the convolutions are not ordered but are more or less incidental to necessities of various pressures within space. And when certain convolutions are pressured into juxta-position, energies are exchanged and phenomena occur that seem inexplicable to the observers of your world.

I know you don't know what we are talking about. If you knew I wouldn't have to be telling you!

Remember we have eliminated the factor of time. Forget it and remember consciousness only. No, you cannot see the physical world or other worlds folded up in accordion pleats or convoluted like a brain. This is not what we are talking about. Patience, child, we will tell it as fast we can. We are discussing True or multi-dimensional space, not a physical world. Of course the world occupies space, but it is not space itself and the air you see between you and the house across the street is not space.

Space is that sphere of influence in which the forces of creation act and have their being.

To say this is True space of sphere of influence is convoluted is exactly so, for it folds back on itself in many ways.

Any event of any nature whatever is encompassed in the extensions/convolutions of True space with all its intermeshed realities.

This is why a true ghost always appears in the same exact place, appears and reappears in the same exact manner, and goes through the same exact formula. Your world has sought for an understanding of such riddles in an understanding of time. They should have sought in space. No real ghost appears out of context to the real event.

The convolutions occur when any event so opposes, thwarts, obstructs, or destructs the natural extension of the laws of creativeness. Space is then driven back on itself, convoluted by the act of non-extension or uncreativeness. Only creative acts spread out through the expanding universe of Reality, thus spreading out True space as it is needed.

The reason you find all this so hard to imagine is that you are accustomed to thinking of reality as something you see with your eyes only. But for example, the true ghosts we were just speaking of and other phenomena related to repetitious events can be actually seen under certain conditions, and through these the convolutions of space are apparent, though not actually seen in themselves.

Specific co-incident convolutions exchange super-charged energies resulting in visual sight. Remember each event in space has intermeshed realities, physical reality, emotional, psychological and others, naming them from your viewpoint. When the emotional stress of an event is very great and that event becomes juxta-positioned to another very emotional event, the interchange of energies super-charges the physical aspects of that event, which permits it to become apparent to physical sight. The various realities of space inter-communicate energy realities. The observation could be other than sight, or other than sight only, such as an audible sound...

We are now communicating through telepathic writing, NOT automatic, and your superconscious is in action, not your subconscious.

In your case the first and physical event and emotional stress was when you used the pendulum with great concentration and came into severe emotional stress of fear of the entities replying to you.

In the convolutions of spatial reality, or in the spreading out of influence of creative forces, a second supercharged emotional psychic stress was juxtapositioned. This second event was the super-tense efforts of the UFO personalities to reach your awareness. Because of your sustained efforts to "make sense out of it all", despite your frequent terrors, there was enough time elapsed, i.e., enough consciousness was put into use, that the interchange of energies (vibratory frequencies) resulted in an excellent development of telepathic abilities.

Is that obscure?

Ah, we knew you would come up with such a question, and were prepared.

"What," you ask, "does the sphere of influence of the creative forces have to do with UFO personalities developing telepathic communication with me? It sounds too complicated and unreal."

Good girl, we wanted you to ask that.

No, it is not because the UFO People are space entities. You are getting off the track and making wild guesses. Okay, you are tired. A little more and we will quit for today.

It is because the UFO people come from an area of influence which is very close to the primal realities of creation. Creative forces are well known phenomena, collaborated with, and understood. Or more simply put,

WE KNOW WHAT IT IS ALL ABOUT!

In contacting Earth we are collaborating with certain elemental forces of Creation to bring about in your world new understanding and cooperation with those natural forces which the world has long neglected.

In the convolutions of True space, we have become neighbors in a way you do not now understand.

We shall return to this writing in a day or so. We all need a little "time out."

Hweig and Co-workers

Creative Forces from Viewpoint of Manifestation

It is upon True space that the record of events is inexorably written as they occur, the so-called Akashic records.

By understanding True (multi-dimensional) space we can reach into these records for whatever we wish to know of the past, which is never truly past but always present.

A puzzling statement at this moment, but to be explained as well as we can devise. Yes, Ida, you have called it the "Forever Now" without actually understanding it. A glimpse only.

We wish True space were as easily defined as True time, and as readily acceptable. It is a very intricate and obscure concept and will require a deal of thought before it becomes acceptable as the fact it is.

There are two factors of True space to be studied and then its relationship to True time to be explored before the whole concept can be seen, so prepare for waiting out the entire revelatory process before abandoning the concept.

We know this will engender negativism, criticism, and non-belief, but bear with our presentation to the end and give it an honest period of consideration and trial. Sooner or later the idea will click. And it will explain so much otherwise inexplicable.

We speak of psychic manifestations or events. This presents opposing viewpoints. From the viewpoint of the happening itself, if it had one, it would be a manifestation. That is, from the viewpoint of someone or some force creating the event it would be a manifestation. From the viewpoint of the observer it would be, naturally, an observed event.

The material given herein will be explicitly and solely from the viewpoint as a manifestation.

We would not know how to explain such psychic doings from the viewpoint of an observed event and since that is the Earth viewpoint – the reflective viewpoint – the people of Earth find it impossible to explain them also.

Now back to the troublesome explanation of True space.

We have said: True space is an elastic medium in which the creative forces act and have their being. You could equally call these Nature forces, though that is more limited as generally used. As the creative forces impel various actions and extension of being, the elastic medium of True space accepts the productions and imprints of these happenings and holds them forever. That is the first factor. The second factor is that True space, the elastic medium, is made up of intermeshed energies of various kinds. From the human viewpoint we could call them emotional, psychic, mental, physical, spiritual etc. This is really not a good description but it will do for a tool right now.

These intermeshed layers of energies must be kept in equilibrium at all times. If a creative happening does not permit balance of all layers, the happening makes a convoluted twist in the fabric of space and indeed True space is more convoluted than any brain.

The second event of a psychic happening is usually a reactionary one to the first event. This is not always so, but a deeper explanation would only confuse what we want to say.

The psychic manifestation of a UFO may be brought about, not incidentally, but deliberately, for we know how to divert the creative forces, and how to utilize True space and True time for our purposes.

The intermeshed energies in True space are indeed alternate worlds.

And this is another revelation. The creative forces, the natural forces are personalities and have "minds" even as you and I. But they must NOT be imagined as persons, or we shall have a whole panoply of great and little gods to propitiate.

But they are personalities and have minds. Why should they not? You do, and you think these are the greatest and best gifts you have. Are they less than you?

Why must these natural forces be thought of as only physical? Is Humanity only physical? Is the life within him physical? His brain yes, but brain is NOT mind: Brain is an interpreter of stimuli, and that is all.

UFO's come from an area of influence very close to the primal realities of creation. Creative forces are well known, acknowledged, collaborated with, understood, and thanked.

So how do we manifest a UFO that isn't there? Or any of our other many manifestations?

We simply find a fold in True space that allows our UFO to become the second happening. It is something like a three dimensional picture, or a moving picture hologram, and here our laser beam comes into use. It is here the psychic existences are needed to provide psychic energies sufficient to make the UFO become physically apparent to the pilot or whoever on the plane, or elsewhere, is in a state of hyper-tension able to perceive it.

We know beforehand who the observer will be, and the whole thing has been staged for his benefit. He has been deliberately brought to a state of tension that will allow his consciousness to accept the manifestation of the "psychic" UFO.

Others with him may not see the manifestation being either not the type of person who would be liable to that type of experience, or not being in a state of hypertension.

Now you ask how an out-of-body experience (OBE) fits into the convoluted space theory. Not a theory, pet, a fact.

The person who has an OBE has a very particular kind of MIND that allows this to occur. His preactive meditation is not true relaxation but a very tight and compact concentration. This creates a mind tension that allows his subconscious level of consciousness to view his experience. Please, no more on this now.

Perhaps we have given enough for the present to allow psychic manifestation and the use of psychic manifestations by the UFO people to at least begin to make a little sense to you and others.

Thank you for your sustained attention,

Hweig and co-workers.

There is one thing we failed to clarify this morning so will take a moment of your time this evening to do so. It is the relationship between stressful event number one and the event juxtapositioned thereto. Actually the second event is not just anything that happens along; it must bear a definite relationship to the first. Usually it is an emotional reaction to the first event. We'll try clarifying this by offering it in capsulated form:

All psychic experiences are engendered by an event of great soul shaking emotion which convolutes space back upon itself, and the second event is usually, though not always, a reaction thereto also involving great emotional stress. Because of the extreme energy exchange between these two events in True space, a psychic manifestation occurs. The third element necessary is consciousness. To bring the manifestation to visibility or audibility or whatever, an observer must be available who could become conscious of that manifestation. (You can find here a parallel to the process your scientists use to make holographic pictures. The two energy exchanges equate to the wave interferences of the holographic process – the consciousness of the observer to the second laser or strong light needed to expose the picture.)

The observer first must be of the type who would be liable to that specific kind of event and he must secondly be in a state of emotional or mental or psychological tension for one reason or another.

A COMPLETELY RELAXED, CALM, UNWORRIED, NON-TENSE SORT OF PERSON SELDOM HAS PSYCHIC EXPERIENCE.

We would need to find out what kind of tension the observer was under. Certain kinds of persons are liable to specific kinds of psychic experience.

There are then three requisites for all psychic manifestations from which the questions in *UFOs and the Psychic Factor* were taken.

1.   An event of great emotional or "soul" impact,

2.   The juxtaposition of a reactional event of great emotional stress, and

3.   The person capable of becoming conscious of that particular type of psychic event.

Ghosts

A "ghost" then is not the spirit of the dead. It is more like a psychic hologram, a three-dimensional picture seen again and again in exactly the same way. "Ghosts" are always repetitious, the same looks, sounds, actions, over and over.

If the "Ghost" seen is not repetitious but goes through varying actions at different times or places, then it is not a true "ghost," but possibly some kind of out-of-body experience of a real living person. There are other possibilities, but we cannot get side-tracked or involved in this now.

The repetitious scene portrayed by the "ghost" need not be the shocking event itself. It seldom is. It is rather an automatic attempt at establishing some of equilibrium (a balancing factor) between events one and two. The "ghost" does not perpetuate it, the alternate event does not manufacture it, but an automatic equalizing occurs, observable only to a consciousness in mental or emotional condition to receive that impression.

Telepathy

Telepathy is the use of the mind energies to direct thoughts into the mind of another. Not all can use it because of factors in their life which cut off the flow of energy, or which blocks the reception thereof.

The particular energy that makes telepathy possible is not yet known to your scientists.

It is akin to electromagnetism, but it is not that.

It lies in the lower part of the brain, a gland that has not been identified carries and controls but does not originate the telepathic current.

To activate this gland a stimulus is required from without. This is usually supplied by another trying to reach a particular person.

Before we can become good telepathic subjects, either sender or receiver, we must learn to relax, both mind and body.

The mysterious energy comes from without. It is a psychic manifestation and that must be studied in depth later.

The psychic connections can only be made by energy existences, at close range. They impel energies to excite and open the centers of telepathy and others to let us see and hear through you. YOU ARE NEVER TOUCHED PHYSICALLY NOR IN-VADED INTERIORLY. It all results from energies directed from the outside.

CHAPTER FOUR

Developing Telepathic Abilities

HWEIG

Telepathy is the ability of one mind to inform another mind of some fact or event.

This information takes place because of certain mind energies, which all persons are heir to but not in the same degree.

Some persons are born with a high capacity far receiving stimuli from other sources. Each person also has limitations, and many limitations are added from their educational environment. They learn not to receive.

Sending or transmitting ability is also inherited, but can be greatly, yes vastly, increased by knowledge and training. Experience and practice are the swiftest routes to becoming a good receiver and a good sender.

Much time has been lost in the past while men pondered whether or no telepathy is a fact. Time is being dissipated now in ingenious experiments to see whether it can be "proven" by decks of cards, picture sending and the like. If more time were spent in developing latent abilities in those most promising ones, a great deal more would be learned, and much faster.

Let us just assume telepathy is a fact without attempting to prove or disprove here. It <u>has</u> been proven elsewhere many, many times. We will not waste time on additional proof.

The fact of telepathy has been established beyond any doubt in scientific studies as well as in staged exhibitions and one proof is just as valid as the other.

Many persons, well endowed with telepathic abilities find themselves participants of strange events for which there can be no other explanation. Popular magazines tell over and over of such experiences.

It is the purpose of this book[0] to outline a program of development for those persons capable and interested in obtaining their best success possible in sending and receiving telepathic messages. Knowledge of what they are doing and practice in doing it are the keynotes of success.

Telepathy has been an instrument in use for unknown centuries. In former times it was more prevalent than today, for people were not so "educated" against it. It will soon become, once again, a common tool.

Before it can be taught, its secrets revealed to the multitudes, there must be a general concession to the necessity to eradicate desires for mis-use. It is, in essence, a kind of mind control, and misused can cause untold misery and many disasters.

The first problem of telepathy is the use to which it is to be put. The second is the integrity of those participating; neither can be of a character liable to misrepresent what is going on, no fabrication, and no elaboration.

Everyone would like to be able to look into or control the mind of his neighbor; no one wants his mind to be the object of invasion by another.

Telepathy is a process by which one mind transfers some of its knowledge to another, or other, minds. The same message can be sent to several others simultaneously if the sender is adept.

As a historical fact, telepathy has been known longer than humanity has been on the face of the Earth. Certain animals have telepathic abilities, notably the dolphins and many subspecies of the primates although the latter has sparse knowledge to transmit. The dolphins and the porpoises, on the other hand, have considerable knowledge and transmit with great skill and purpose. In fact we shall later devote an entire chapter to animals on Earth and their telepathic abilities.

But, back to Humanity. At this place in time he has all but lost his capacity to receive and ability to transmit telepathically. His psychic centers have been unused for so long they lie dormant with the threat of atrophy if they are not soon awakened and used and developed.

The purpose of this writing is to convey the knowledge of telepathy, its causes, its resources, its aims.

Once, Humanity on Earth used his capacities with great skill, as great as that of the dolphins (!) but the control fell into the hands of an elite group who forbade its use by the common people. Gradually the skill was forgotten; children never developed the disciplines necessary to its use. Then, even the control class slowly allowed the development to become corroded with stupid practices carried out mainly to impress the gullible and timid.

Telepathy became a weapon of power, its secrets became more and more exclusive until only a few were taught in each generation and at last the knowledge slowly seeped away into the sands of time.

Telepathy is merely a lost art. It can be relearned by all with the inherent capacity and the willingness to undergo the disciplines necessary to its development.

Heredity is the opening factor. All men are not born equal as far as capacities and limitations of the mind are concerned. They are born exquisitely unequal and it is upon this inequality that the castles of the mind are built.

The races of men are so mixed and confused by this time that factors of equality and inequality can in no way be determined by race alone, but mainly by the individual.

There is no way to make such distinctions easily or quickly. A certain shape of the head or tilt of the nose tells us nothing. The manner of thinking of an individual is the quickest clue to his capacity for reception and transmission of telepathic knowledge.

One chapter will be devoted to a questionnaire by which individual probability of success in telepathy can be somewhat determined, at least in aptitude. Only long and sustained trial and error can determine the extent to which the art can be developed in any individual, a step-by-step process with no way to tell the final result until it has been reached.

In the early days of Humankind on Earth, and he did not originate on Earth, nor did he develop from Earth's animals, a subject surely controversial but to be shown and proven in a later book, but in his early days on Earth humans knew little "intellectual" conversation. Sophisticated and subtle nuances of meaning were not developed; therefore word symbols were not as necessary as they were later. Visualizing what was happening or to happen or hope to happen was the swiftest and simplest process of thought. As the human brain became more sophisticated word symbology became a necessity. Communication began with monosyllables and gestures, but all the while pictorial representation still flashed in the mind of the speaker, and when, still later, men wanted to leave a written message or instruction for those who followed, he first "wrote" them to correspond to the picture in his mind. Alphabetical spelling of words was a very long and slow development in human communication. Among some peoples, as the Chinese and Japanese, an alphabet was never invented. Their Kanji or word symbols all derive from pictorial representations.

Now the psychic centers that allow the fact of telepathy to exist have been so long unused that their location, function, and attributes have been forgotten.

There are seven psychic centers in the physical brain of Man. They cannot be detected by the scalpel or by chemical analysis. They can be detected only by use.

These seven psychic centers control such psychic phenomena as telepathy, hypnosis, dreams, soul travel, levitation, psychic imagery (visions), prognostication, clairvoyance, clairaudience, and hundreds of other psychic phenomena, many of which are not recognized as being of psychic origin.

This writing shall deal mainly with telepathy with only a reference now and then to hypnosis, which is very closely connected. The next writing shall deal mainly with hypnosis, (a human power grossly misunderstood, misused, and unused).

The people of Atlantis knew and used all of the psychic powers to a masterful degree. After the self-destruction of Atlantis the remaining few spread in small groups over the Earth taking their knowledge with them. These groups, infiltrating and finally becoming absorbed in less developed races, found it impossible to keep their powers secret. As their knowledge was revealed it was distorted, prostituted, condemned by emotional zealots who feared losing their own power of submission of the common people. Finally the practices of the Masters had degenerated into Magic as stage show trickery to impress moronic audiences. The Masters themselves were long gone, a "vanished" race, vanished into the mixed bloodlines of the less developed peoples. Atlantis was truly "dead" when the last of the Masters departed from life.

Ritual was left, empty rituals and initiations and self-select groups trying to put over dead mummery as live powers.

And after so long a time even the belief in Magic died, although here and there a spark was occasionally struck from the dead ashes of the ancient knowledge.

Today, studies in parapsychology and other disciplines and experiments are beginning to blow a breath of life into the long dead practice of psychic manifestation. More and more persons of scientific and adventurous bent are becoming intensely interested in the various phenomena.

Perhaps this is the time the psychic discipline of Telepathy should once again be given to Earth, as it was in the dawn of Humankind.

CHAPTER FIVE

The UFO Contactee Experience

IDA M. KANNENBERG

For years I have had an on-going telepathic contact with a personality who claims to be of the UFO fraternity. This telepathic friend and comrade, Hweig as he names himself, has said he was born on Earth of a Russian mother and a "UFO fly- by-night" father.

When Hweig was seven his mother died and the UFO people came and took him to another planet where he was reared and educated in their knowledge and their life customs?[1]

In our year 1940 Hweig came back to Earth, not too well prompted in what he would find.

Night of the Flaming Moon

It has taken me many years to recall events and to garner information as to the exact time, place, and names pertaining to my experience, which took place on that same cold, dark, mysterious night, when Hweig came home. Tom Mitchell was driving the 1939 Dodge four-door sedan that conveyed Army Corporal Jerry Smith, then 22 years of age, my husband Dave, and I was 26. This was a share-the ride trip. Dave and I were on the way to my sister's house in Phoenix for Christmas.

---

[1] *A Son Of Old Atlantis* is Hweig's autobiography.

We four had left a little cafe in Indio at 9:20 p.m. on December 22, 1940, heading east on old highway 10 in southern California. I looked at my watch on leaving the cafe and thought "I must remember this time." Then I thought, "But that's silly! Why would I ever want to remember the time?"

We were 30 miles past Desert Center and about 18 miles outside of Blythe. The old road was much more twisting and uneven than Interstate 10 that now passes that way. It was a detour while the main road was being improved.

As we came over a little rise a little after 11:00 p.m., a deep glow spread over the desert before us. On the horizon appeared a flaming orange-red crescent that grew rapidly into an ellipse and became a deeper blood-red hue. At first we thought it was the full moon rising, but it did not behave properly. It seemed to spring from the horizon and hurl itself towards us.

"My God! What is that?" cried Jerry.

"That's no moon!" I said, my voice quaking.

We turned from our northeasterly direction into an easterly one. An intervening mountain range shut off our view. Then the object, now rounded into a flaming red ball, seemed to sidle to the left from behind the obstructing hills - at ground level! We paralleled the hill, traveling right and beyond.

Tom pulled the car into a wide turnout. He touched Dave on the shoulder and said to Jerry, "Come on."

The three men went down the road and stood talking in the headlights at great length. The glow was gone. It was dark, cold, and wet from heavy rains. Still the men talked. I wrapped myself more tightly in my blanket and thought I dozed.

I did not know what happened next until 40 years later. In 1980 I went under regressive hypnosis with Dr. R. Leo Sprinkle at the University of Wyoming. This part will be revealed in its proper sequence.

Mental Telepathy

My excursion into the development of mental telepathy began first in 1968. I was introduced to the use of a pendulum by a young woman with whom I had worked. I began to experiment with a paper clip and a piece of sewing thread for a pendulum. I made vertical and horizontal lines to get "yes" and "no" answers to my questions. Presently I enlarged upon the scheme by drawing a six-inch circle and writing the letters of the alphabet around it. Now the pendulum answered my questions with full responses! I would not recommend this, since it can be as dangerous as the Ouija board as I too soon found out.

Such concentration it took! And that was the opening door. Long later I came to realize, too late, that by such full concentration to the oblivion of everything else, I was hypnotizing myself and making myself open to what became telepathic communication.

One night as I sat using the pendulum I heard a group of men talking, as clearly as though they had been in the next room.

One said, "Will you drop this off for me on your way down to the office in the morning?"

There were several other statements I do not recall.

Then one said, "Do you remember the little girl under the lilac tree?"

And a wonderful, deep voice said, "Wait! She is beginning to hear us now!"

The voices cut off abruptly, as though a door had been silently but firmly closed.

Soon I was not just watching the pendulum spell out words, I was actually hearing them in my mind! But there seemed to be conflict of some kind, as though two different factions were vying for my attention

After some weeks, the telepathy became actual voices whispering in my ear. One of the two factions became threatening, and seemed to delight in telling me what dire things were about to happen to me, until, thoroughly terrorized, I wound up in a hospital.

For several days in the hospital the dire voices were still there, cajoling me to run through the doors.

But there came a powerful voice that said, *"Leave this woman alone!"*

Silence, then the faintest whisper, "Ida! *Who are you?*" Back in the days when things were merely silly and rather fun, both the pendulum and later the whispers had asked many times, "Who are you?"

I could never understand why they should ask this. Why should it be necessary? They had chosen to communicate with me. They must have some knowledge of me. I tried to answer this question with my name, address, facts of my life and background. They always said, "We know all that! *But who are you?*"

So once again I gave the only answer I had, "Ida," I said. "Just Ida. That's all I know."

After all this it was probably a day and a half before I realized the whispering voices were gone. I never heard them again. Soon I was back home running my little antique shop.

It was nine years, November 1977, before I gained enough courage and emotional equilibrium to take up the pendulum again. First there was simply the pointing to letters in answer to my questions, then the telepathic words came into my mind

Now "they" could talk to me at any time and just by thinking I was opening my mind for them to receive my thoughts. I certainly did not like this invasion of privacy.

Soon they said, "Get a pencil." There were a few days of automatic writing, and then I realized I was hearing the words before I wrote them down. Soon telepathic writing and conversation were firmly established. For a long time I was questioning and skeptical of this telepathic contact, seemingly thrust upon me from nowhere, without rhyme or reason.

My first skepticism was directed towards myself. Was I experiencing something like a split personality? Had I invented a Tulpa, an imaginary personality that becomes so strong it is almost real? Was my subconscious out of kilter and playing tricks on me? Was I simply going nuts?

It took three years just to satisfy myself that these constant telepathic personalities, who gave themselves various names, were totally real, in *some* condition of reality, and most vital of all, that they existed completely outside of myself. They were in no way part of me, nor was I part of them. I had not invented nor produced them by some process of dissociation. Once I was sure of myself, my skepticism centered on them, my communicators.

Were they truly who they pretended to be, all "human" personalities, though in various life forms? Were their purposes what they said they intended to help the people of this planet come to a better understanding of themselves and of the good earth?

After more than ten years of this contact I have to admit that I have had too many evidences of their reality to doubt them, or myself, any longer. Yet these evidences are so subjective, so personal, I would have difficulty trying to convince anyone else. But I would like to share with you some of the dictation as received.

What

Once I brought up the subject of UFO's and the dictated answer was: "UFOs exist and are not to be taken lightly. They pose no threat at present. We can only say they are being surveyed by earth scientists, but secretly. There exist excellent photos in several European countries and in the United States as well. Some UFOs are manufactured objects of physical elements; some are not. The physical ones originate on several planets outside your solar system. They are based on Earth under the sea.

"We were working with new tools last time and none of us were adept enough to block interference. We lost control to others. Everyone was appalled when you became ill and a halt was called to such activity for a long time until you were emotionally ready, and we were better practiced in our part of the work.

"There are instances in which persons like yourself were given information that they used to the disadvantage of others. This cannot be permitted. Therefore, we must proceed slowly and cautiously, testing frequently for results we do not wish. We know you understand.

"We are able to draw upon the wisdom that has been lost to your world through destruction by idiots and the prohibition of idiot authorities against the use of talents you otherwise never would have lost. Telepathy is one of those talents.

"You are slightly dissociated, just enough to keep two levels of awareness on stage at all times. You are not, however, using your subconscious, but your superconscious, for that is our area of activity at the present time. We can and do have another area of activity, which will shortly be brought into your knowledge. It is an important one for which this preliminary work has been preparing you. A great surprise is in store for you, and we hope you will be as thrilled as we are to present it to you. Patience, a few days only.

"We are the originators of the UFO's as you call them. Some of the UFOs are energy manifestations. We mentioned this once before, or rather how we materialize for our own use whatever we need.

"That is not the full story, by far. We are just human as you are, and just as corporeal. We are also masters of all psychic phenomena.

"You wonder why we can converse so easily in your own kind of speech. Our language is mostly pictorial telepathy with each other, but there is a person who is able to translate for us and acts as interpreter for all our messages. We transmit through Mordalla. It is translated and relayed on your side by one who calls himself *Hweig!*

"You have wondered why much of what we tell you sounds like feedback from things you have told or shown or read for us. There is good reason for this, the transmission of ideas by direct verbal telepathy. We can use only the words and visual experiences you have in your mind already for this kind of contact. If we tried to explain something totally new to you, we would have to use pictorial telepathy and that takes a lot of preparation. No, not even Hweig can translate except in terms you already recognize.

"A great number of our scientists now work with persons here on Earth, trying to bring them to a condition of usefulness for the purpose of making direct contact and physical landings. Your people are not emotionally prepared for us, not nearly as much as we had hoped.

"We have come to the conclusion that the only way we can make direct contact without being shot down is by revealing truths about ourselves. By doing it in such a manner as this, we are not putting our lives in jeopardy

"We want to emphasize the difference between psychic and spiritual. We never dreamed there could be so much confusion between the two! We, the UFO people, deal in psychic matters.

There are others who bring you information on spiritual matters. This does not concern us, except to warn you not to allow a cult or religion to arise based on what we tell you. No cults! No religions!

"The vibrations of your voice are an energy transmission to which we are tuned with our psychic receivers, which you have as well, but don't know how to use yet. You will be taught.

"At first, the vibrations of voice are necessary. Later, after we have learned your mode of speech and connotations, which are different for each, you will be able to transmit thought vibrations without the actual voice. You will not realize what or how you are doing this until we have time to teach you more about it. Either kind of vibration is picked up by us and translated into symbols regardless of your language or any impediment of speech. Actually it is the energy pattern of thought that comes through. At first, these patterns are registered by a chart or graph. (We have a permanent record of what you think!) Once we have learned your particular thought patterns and their meanings, we can receive them directly into our minds, even as you are transmitting them directly from your mind. A perfect telepathy has been established. All of this is much simpler than our labored explanation sounds.

"Automatic writing may start before you are able to receive our communication in return. Once telepathy has been established then the automatic writing can turn to telepathic writing which seems to be nothing more nor less than dictation from us. Whatever the exact process proves to be for each of you, we are soon conversing in your own vernacular or idiom, either by pen or voice, or both.

"By that time we have been able to measure very accurately your potential use to us and to your fellow man. We have a pretty good understanding of your potentials as psychic researchers and a profound judgment of your character.

"We cannot judge entirely beforehand how any contactee will respond to our approaches, therefore tentative and elusive contacts of different kinds must be made previous to the big open vital contact. Sometimes years are spent in this getting- acquainted routine before we dare expose ourselves in an open confrontation.

"Many hours are spent in analyzing, planning, judging, and re-planning, changing our tactics constantly as necessity demands.

"The major portion of our planning time is spent in evaluating that particular and specific pattern of beliefs the developing individual seems loathe to abandon as he matures.

"Therefore we build our design around this particular person's belief in his own worth. It is amazing how many people have little confidence in their own value. Their self-esteem has been squashed by life events at an early age.

"Our first task is to put our contactee through a series of self-experiences that allows him to see himself as a worthy person [with] potential [for] prideful accomplishments and gratifying attainments.

"Through our manipulations we persuade him to run over in his mind all the mistakes and errors of his past. He finds himself picking through these painful memories and examining them thoroughly one by one, in the light of his later years. A kind of mental catharsis takes place relieving him of his self-condemnation and profound regret for events past that he felt should have been better handled. He begins to see he has not been all bad, or wicked, or gauche.

"After our contactee is well on the way to forgiving himself for all his supposed crimes, misdemeanors, [and] silly mistakes and has begun to revalue his basic beliefs, we begin to work on his dependency on others. This is an even tougher battle, for life has taught him more about his weaknesses than his strengths, and has led him to lean heavily or lightly on the broad shoulders and strong back of some figure, more or less heroic to him, to him he gives allegiance, and too often, his own strength. To wean him from that dependency and to bring him (or her) to rely on his own strength is a most difficult and wearying task. Therefore, he is led to many events which expose him to himself, to make him aware of what he is, and more important, of what he can be. Always the choice is his, his free will is not hindered, but he is made aware, through experience, by passing through events, not by preaching. Some of the events, indeed many, are hurtful, not because we wish to be mean, but because we wish a change to take place. Preaching can never produce the change that experience can.

"Thus we put him into new activities, new adventures, new contacts, and exposure to new ideas from which arises his opportunities to change, to expand his pattern of beliefs.

"We maneuver and manipulate and expose him to the forces of change in every way we can. But never to the point of smothering or obstructing his free will. He chooses according to what he is and what he will be.

"And we plant seemingly insignificant factors in his life that will be essential to something very important in his future. Thus we begin to find and tie together all the threads that will weave the fabric of his refined basic beliefs.

"Those contactees who elevate themselves without true reason and find themselves unable to come down from their ego fling are left right there, babbling forever about past glories and advancing not one step further in the direction of human evolution or collaborating with the cosmic forces and principles which guide them as well as ourselves. They are left to flutter helplessly in the breeze of their own blasts of non-comprehension. Such persons give a bad reputation to the whole course of UFO-contactee experiences. Unfortunately the most comprehending and best evolving contactees are usually the most quiet and unobtrusive. The bombastic rhetoric of the "fallen angels" obscure and distort the calm exploration and valuable observations of the staid and steady.

"Once our contactee has reached self-esteem and self-de- pendency we can hope to bolster his self-assurance. This means he becomes convinced of the rightness of his activities, his choice, his path, his responsibilities, his duties. Becoming definitely convinced of these he can now march firmly forward into collaboration with us, giving of his best potentials and reaffirming his faith in himself at every step.

"There remains one further step and that is to free himself of all that would hinder his march to his own destiny. He must not abandon his task for the sake of some clinging demand from others. He must become wise as well as patient to consider and re-consider what is necessary and advantageous to his course, and what is confining and obscuring or hindering.

Some of his most cherished and basic beliefs must be reexamined from the viewpoint of his "new self. Some of his strongest ties must be loosened. This does not mean abandoning family or friends or social responsibilities. It means careful measuring of time and talents to give each its just and honorable due, but no more. No sacrificing of one to the other, simply a reweighing, remeasuring, readjusting, a budgeting of time and purpose. This is the most difficult of all his assignments, but it must be thoroughly done before he can step out confidently and surely upon the path we have selected for him, and which, in the long run, he has chosen for himself."

How

The foregoing dictation tells us *what* they do relative to interaction with their contactees, but *how* do they do it? Through what methods do they accomplish their purposes? Let us return to some additional dictation.

"We, the people of the UFO's, speak to the respected inhabitants of the Planet Earth to explain the methods we have used to make contacts with them.

"Due to our lack of knowledge of the Earth people, to our haste in trying to make contacts, and the fear and sometimes aggressiveness with which we were met, we have made many errors. We ask for leniency of judgment until we have had an opportunity to present ourselves in a more circumspect manner.

"First let us speak of the manner or manners in which we are seen or otherwise make ourselves known:

"Actual physical craft and human or humanoid (as you call them) occupants are seen or encountered.

"Hallucinatory craft and occupants due to the hypnosis of the contactees are seen or encountered.

"Craft/personalities are unseen, but their presence detected. These are psychic manifestations.

"Remote contact by telepathy and other means, mostly MECHANICAL.

"More immediate and personal contacts by means we cannot reveal at this time.

"We choose contactees long in advance, no contact is accidental. We choose illusory experiences to fit the contactee.

Our intentions are for the contactee to come forward at certain times in the future, with acknowledgment of the incident. Sometimes, due to psychological accidents they remember too soon.

"Remember at all times our intentions are beneficial and our desires peaceable.

Types of Manifestations

"Psychic manifestations are used by the people of the UFO's. To begin with, our manifestations are most carefully adapted to the suitability of the occasions and the understanding of the contactee.

"Manifestations fall roughly into five major categories with a multitude of sub-varieties. Here we can speak only of the most significant ones:

"Manifestations of a semi-corporeal self. We manifest ourselves in what to all appearances is as physical and corporeal as yourselves, but if you touched us with any material object we would simply not be there. You could walk right through us. We are only semi-corporeal, visibly and audibly so, but with a corporeality much different than your own, not as dense, and of a "substance" of a much higher vibratory rate.

"Manifestations of craft in the same degree of semi-corporeality. To all appearances it is there, but it can disappear in a second and can seemingly reappear instantaneously a great distance away.

"Manifestations of events through auditory sounds and/or visual scenes. You would stake your life that you heard or saw something, and in a deeper sense you did, but it was not there in the physical-vibratory sense. Persons who walk through the garden of Versailles and seem to find themselves back in the days of Marie Antoinette are seeing a visual manifestation of this kind. (But this one is not from us).

"Manifestations of something physical being done to yourself. If you accept this without fear, there will be no adverse effect, not even pain. To struggle against it in fear creates pain and mental anguish. (We must note that actual physical interaction can and often does create real pain).

"All of these first four manifestations seem very solid, real, factual, and physical but ALL are another form of hallucination, an illusionary experience. But the impact on the percipient, the end result, is just as real as though it were all physical and factual.

"We use the psychic manifestation for one main reason; there are also several minor reasons:

"It is easier to devise these illusory experiences than it is to send a craft or persons from our planet, or to engineer a real event, and the results are absolutely the same! If the contactee went through the experience, or only thought he went through the experience, the end result is exactly the same. What we seek is interaction and reaction of the contactee. In certain instances then, illusion serves just as valid a purpose as actuality!

"To obtain other ends, accomplish other purposes on other occasions, we must resort to actual physical events, and appear in actual hardware craft, and in our actual corporeal physical being. To interact physically with you we must appear in our physical selves.

"Now to category 5: We enter your world in the out-of-body state as you call it. We are, then, totally invisible, though we can take on semi-corporeality instantaneously if we wish.

As psychic masters we can move in and out of these states at will and have complete control of our intent and actions. Now, lest all this alarm you unduly, we must add: we cannot do all this idly or for your personal purposes or amusement. Laws governing our actions are most stringent. To use these abilities in your world requires special sanctions for use on specific occasions only.

"Our purpose in coming in this invisible state is to establish communication with as many earth persons as possible, to develop telepathic contacts with those capable, and to find out for ourselves what we can of the nature and ways of Earth beings.

"We, too, look to higher forces for guidance, and our punishment is swift and inevitable if we use our powers arbitrarily or for unsanctioned purposes.

"*We are part of a great plan. We are sent to inform and make aware!*"

I have received many hundreds of pages of such dictation.

Regression

Now we return to that dark night of December 22, 1940 on the California desert when we saw the flaming object that turned into a great red ball that sidled out from behind the hill. We left me trying to doze while Tom, Jerry and Dave stood in the road talking.

In 1980 I went to Laramie, Wyoming, where Dr. Leo Sprinkle put me into regressive hypnosis and for the first time I learned I had truly been on an alien craft. A partial picture of the subsequent events emerged at that session, and recently many bits of recall have filled in that picture. More are still coming.

As I huddled in my blanket I heard the scrunching of footsteps and thought, "Good. The men are coming back." We had driven straight through from Bremerton, Washington, and were all tired and groggy.

The back door opened and a blast of cold air hit me. I wondered why the front doors did not open and why no one was saying anything. I sat up and looked ahead. My three men were still standing in the road, a good distance from the car.

The man who held the door open was a stranger. I could not see well in the darkness.

"We need help," the stranger said, "Come help us?"

I was startled and apprehensive and said quickly with a quaver in my voice, "I will get the men. They are right there in front of the car.

A second man leaned forward. "We don't want the men," he said. "We need a woman."

The first man was speaking at the same time. "There has been an accident. Can you help?"

I thought they meant a car accident and maybe they needed a woman to deal with a miscarriage that had resulted.

Under hypnosis I reported that the first man added that someone needed a blood transfusion, although I do not consciously remember this part of the conversation. I said my type might not work, since it is a rare type. They said they knew my type and it was OK. Much later they told me that this conversation was only a ploy to make me go with them.

The second man said, "It will only take a few minutes. The men will never miss you."

I went with them. I remember walking in the gravelly, sandy soil, stumbling a little in the dark. Everything was deadly silent, as though we walked in a vacuum. The two men walked at either side and a little behind, as though herding me.

Once my foot rolled on a pebble; I lurched forward. The first man gently put his hand under my left elbow to steady me. We came to what I thought was a round cabin. I wondered what a cabin was doing way out there, so far from everything. A door stood open, a yellowish light shone out. At the entrance someone said, "Step up. There is a high step here."

I tried to step up with my right foot and couldn't quite make it. As I tried my left foot a man in a tan uniform leaned down and caught my right wrist and literally, but gently, yanked me into the "cabin."

My conscious memories stop here. Try as I might, I cannot consciously recall past that high step. From this point the story derives from the hypnosis session with Dr. Sprinkle.

Inside it was light. Everything was whitish metal. I sat on a high stool. There were five men who looked human, like us. They were taller than I. Someone took blood from my left arm with a big syringe. One man was injured in the chest and bleeding. He was shorter, lying down, and covered with a metallic blanket. I could not see much of him. It was Hweig who had fallen and hurt himself, but not as badly as they made it appear to me. Only one man spoke to me in English, with no discernable accent. He thanked me and asked me to help in other ways. They wanted to communicate with me again. They pressed something way into each ear, and it hurt. They pressed something into my left nostril. I could not see what it was. It went way up into my nose and hurt, but not too badly. They said they would contact me much later so that I could help them again. This is the extent of this part of the hypnosis session.

Later I learned the nose and eye implants allow them to "see through my eyes and hear through my ears," as they have assured me many times that they are able to do. Later it became apparent that there must have been a brain implant made at the same time. It may have been through the eye socket, like a lobotomy. The brain implant allows them to control the entire muscular system of my body.

They took me back to the car, which I do not remember at all. Later I awoke from my doze and looked at my watch. It was twenty minutes past midnight. I heard the men coming back. I thought, "That's funny. I thought they came back once before." I decided I had dreamed it.

Jerry got into the car shivering and shaking. "If I had known we were going to be out there this long I would have worn my jacket," he said. The other two conferred and decided we had stopped close to an hour. They seemed surprised. They said that if a truck stop were open we would get hot coffee in Blythe.

As we drove on, a huge silvery disk rose above the trees on our left. I remarked how rapidly it was shooting up. One of the men said, "You see, it was only the moon."

About 2:20 a.m. I awoke from another doze. High in the sky was a glistening moon, a little less than quarter full. I called it to the men's attention, but they seemed not to want to discuss it. I watched it for more than 10 minutes, then went back to sleep.

The next day I found Dave sitting alone in the living room at my sister's house. He was a very gregarious man and would never sit alone if there were even a cat to talk to. He was gnawing on his knuckles. I asked him what was so important to discuss that the men had stood so long in the road - out of my hearing. He was reluctant to say anything, but finally said, "Oh, nothing. Nothing important." Tom had been working in the Bremerton Navy Yard and had already taken preliminary Air Force training. Is it possible he had heard of UFO's - whatever they were called then, and that is why he had taken the men to talk?

Later I was told that the men had been frozen by hypnosis in the road while I was being taken to the craft, and that afterward my husband had only a vague recollection that they had left the car or had stood so long talking. It has taken years to check all of these details and to return to the area to take pictures. Meteorological records for December 22 show that the proper moon was a quarter moon, just as I recall watching it later that night. My conscious memory will not yet allow me to see the whole story. I am sure there is more, but I try not to force recall, for fear that dwelling upon it may cause me to fantasize.

It must come of its own accord, just as Hweig first came to me that dark and mysterious night in 1940.

Remember When...

When I went under regressive hypnosis in 1980, there was another event I wanted to examine. I have already told you about the night of the flaming moon.

My communicators were beginning to nag me to "remember when you were a little girl playing under the lilac tree." I could not remember this.

I thought and thought for days, but not an inkling came through. One day I was looking through an old photo album of my mother's, and I came upon a snapshot taken that very day and place - myself under the lilac tree! Then the memory returned swiftly. So at the hypnosis session I asked Dr. Sprinkle to regress me to that place and time. What follows is the story that emerged from my regression:

We were living in Davenport, Iowa, and I was going home on Carey Avenue. I was thinking of bringing my mother some violets or lilacs, but they were all gone. All I found was garter snakes. I decided to lie down under the lilac bush for a while.

I heard someone's footsteps approaching in the grass, so I sat up. I hadn't worn my glasses out to play, so I could not see very well. There were two men in business suits. One man was bigger, with gray hair. The other was a younger man and smaller.

"Do you know Mr. Barton?" they asked.

"Yes, the blind man," I replied.

"Doesn't he live around here somewhere?" one asked me.

"Right there. That house."

"This one right here?"

"Yes," I answered.

The men talked together, but I could not hear them very clearly. The younger one spoke only to the older man, who in turn spoke to me.

"What is your name," he asked. "Where do you live? What does your father do? Where do you go to school? Do you like school?"

Next, the older man started talking to me in a way that I heard inside my head, without my ears hearing. Only under this regression were the words realized.

"You will need to know all about people," he said inside my head. "Why they act as they do. What do they mean besides what they say? You will learn to write well. Try harder at your spelling. Learn about grammar. Make nice sentences. Someday you will write many wonderful, unknown things. We will see you again when you are grown up and much older."

Then out loud he said, "Be a good girl." They went over to their car, which was parked on the wrong side of the street, as if they didn't know any better. They never did visit Mr. Barton.

Later I read in the story of another contactee that the alien who contacted him said, "While I am talking to you, I am also putting things into your mind. We do that with all our contactees."

And still much later I was told that the two men who spoke to me under the lilac tree were Amorto and Jamie, and that they were the same two who took me from the car in 1940 and into the UFO. I usually refer to Amorto, Jamie, Hweig and their colleagues as "Hweig & Co."

Living with Hweig

During these past ten years my personal relationship with Hweig, who has become a sort of live-in companion, has mellowed from the first fear-filled reaction to his presence into one of camaraderie and friendship.

We have had some awfully good and sometimes awfully funny telepathic sessions.

I cannot dislodge him, no matter what I do. I have begged, pleaded, wept, threatened, and screamed, "Get the hell out of my life!" but after reaching many compromises, we are still together. He makes me laugh when I am dull and makes commiserating noises when I am sad. Most of all, he encourages me to keep writing. "Get the word out," he says. "Tell people that contactees are in the position they are through no fault of their own. They have not negotiated their strange and bizarre experiences for the sake of getting attention."

Believe me, we contactees could get attention in a lot less stressful and painful ways, if that was what we were after!

Contactees may not have all the answers, but careful observation and analysis of the contactee experience can lead any concerned scientist to some of the answers of the mysteries of the UFO phenomenon.

Hweig has proven himself useful in many ways, in finding things for me. When I have misplaced something, searched and given up, I say, "O.K., Hweig, where did I leave my brown gloves?" Then I write or read or watch TV for a few minutes. Presently I get up, walk to a drawer, stick my hand inside without looking and pull out the gloves.

"Actually," says Hweig, "your subconscious remembers where you put the gloves. I only give a little boost to action, to get you off your duff and into the other room."

He has helped me on more than one occasion to find something interesting I otherwise would have overlooked. Once my granddaughter and I were playing along a little stream, way out in the country. We found some smooth round rocks about fist size that had been blackened and cracked by fire.

"Maybe these have been used by Indians to boil their stew," I said. "Let's look around."

We found a few stones that looked as though they had been used to pound with, but nothing really exciting.

"It's getting late. We'd better go," I said.

"Wait," said Hweig. There is something you have overlooked. Go upstream a little."

I went and found nothing. "We gotta go."

"No! A little further. Use your eyes!"

Still nothing.

"Just a little more," coaxed Hweig.

I went a few feet and stopped. "This is as far as I am going," I said.

"Then, look!" He said.

So I looked. Out in the middle of the stream was a rock the size of a small dishpan. The sides were rounded, but the bottom that was sticking up was flat as a table and on a slant. I waded out and turned it over. It was a metate, a millstone for hand grinding of grains.

"How did you know that was there?" I asked.

"Things are not always as mysterious or miraculous as you try to make them," he said smugly. "I saw it when you were down this direction a while ago."

"How did you know it was a metate? It was upside down."

"Hweig knows many things," he said primly. And that was that.

Hweig is useful. He wakes me up at whatever time I have asked him to, right on the dot. Sometimes I don't want to get up.

"Come on," says Hweig. "We have a lot to do today."

"I don't wanna."

The next thing I know my feet hit the floor. I have battled him on this one, but he always wins. Sometimes I am halfway downstairs before I realize I'm up.

Sometimes he steers me into bookstores and directly to a book I don't even know I want to buy. I have been on the bus going home before I look to see what the title is of the book I just bought.

It worries me often, that he can prod me into doing things that seem not to be of my own volition.

"You are functioning on three levels of awareness," Hweig explains. "It is you, truly, who do these things from your subconscious and your superconscious, but your conscious level is not aware of all the factors."

This is like walking around two-thirds deaf, mute and blind, and not knowing it.

I said, "It is nice to know one has the ability. But what am I supposed to do with it?"

"Absorb," says Hweig. "Just absorb."

As though I were a sponge!

You can tell, I am sure, that Hweig and I do a lot of arguing. I am not complacent, a pawn, a robot. I suppose he is guiding my development into strange and only partially realized directions.

Hweig is almost unbearably patient. When I throw a temper fit he merely sighs and waits. When I get all through stamping my feet and yelling he goes right on from where he left off as though nothing has intervened. Since I don't get any response from a tantrum I don't subject myself to the wear and tear anymore. An expletive will let him know my reaction just as well. Then we both sigh and go on from there. He just about has me broken to harness.

When I first had this mental contact with Hweig he was collecting puns. He became bored with that and, after listening to my mother, began to collect what he called "folk omens."

"If a broom falls across the door you will have company." "If you put two dinner knives at the same plate, you will cut a friendship."

"If you sing before you eat, you'll cry before you sleep." But Hweig's all-time favorite is, "If your nose itches you've been sticking it into someone else's business."

He says he is still collecting folk omens, and from all over the world. If he ever publishes his collection, he will dedicate it to my mother.

Now doesn't he sound just like what he declares himself to be, a very human fellow, just as physical and corporeal as ourselves?

I ask him, "If you are so human and physical, where do you live? I would like to send you a Christmas card."

He laughs and says, "Oh, I travel around a lot. I've lived in many places. Right now I am living in San Francisco."

He allows me to see a mental picture of his living quarters. I would recognize the house should I see it. There are always sea gulls swirling about. I think it is in an area not far from Golden Gate Park. His apartment is on the third floor of a late Victorian house and has been remodeled from two former apartments. I see a grand piano and ask him if he plays.

"Like a concert pianist," he says modestly. "Or I could if I had ten fingers. I have only four digits on each hand and must modify the music."

He further describes himself as being five feet four inches tall, very broad of shoulder, with eyes blue as the skies. I think I would know him, too, should I ever meet him again, though I do not recall his looks from our brief meeting in 1940. Once I told him, "If you are a real physical person as you say you are, living in the United States, and I should ever meet you, I am going to march right up to you and poke you in the nose for all the mischief that you have given me."

"If you do," said Hweig sweetly, "I will turn you over my knee and spank you."

I am not offering these anecdotes just to talk about myself. I am reporting facts of experience. I am not an accredited scientist, but as the one who had the experiences, and one who has enjoyed or suffered the *effects* of these experiences, I feel I am fully qualified and licensed to *analyze the facts.*

Such experiences can be physical, mental, or even illusionary. Experience is experience. These are the facts and the analysis thereof.

UFO Sleuthing

One of the most profound books ever written about UFO's and contactees was Dr. Jacques Vallee's *Messengers of Deception.* He said a great many wise, revealing and perceptive things, though he was not altogether flattering to the victims of the events, the contactees.

One thing he said sent me off into a different type of study. "Scientists," said Dr. Vallee, "may be in the same situation with UFO's as they are with crime; every police department has a criminology lab, but it is the *detective* who finds the criminal, not the technician. *Where are the UFO detectives?*"

Here, I hope, is one.

Since I inherited from my mother a certain sleuthing ability - she was a super sleuth - she knew everything that was going on in the neighborhood and she never left the house - I thought I would try a little detective work on the UFO situation.

What does a detective concentrate on first? He finds the modus operandi, the pattern of operation of the one perpetrating the mischief.

In this case he finds the *master minds* behind the advent of the UFO's and of the contacts purporting to be of UFO origin - not the craft, not the operators, not the occupants thereof, these are the workers - but he finds the *planners* of the whole event.

Each contactee is a unique individual and his specific experiences are unique to himself. But on closer observation, underneath that individuality, a pattern becomes apparent. It solves nothing to say the contactees create the pattern themselves in that they are naive and gullible and looking for salvation from the stars.

As one who has suffered through many, many such patterns, one who is not altogether naive and gullible, and who is, to Hweig's great despair, still pretty skeptical and rebellious, I can safely declare the patterns are imposed through various machinations of the UFO planners and those who execute their orders.

Consider first the pattern of the name game. In my early telepathic contact I was told I would be called Rama rather than using my own name. I fussed about this. I am Ida. I like being Ida. I try to be the best Ida I can be. I did not want, I did not intend to be anybody's Rama.

Perhaps it was because I fussed so much that Hweig later told me to forget the name Rama, to go back through all my notes and writing and to change the name to Ida in every instance. From that time on they have called me only by my proper name. As I began to correspond and to meet other contactees, quite a lot of them, I discovered many admitted to having been given another name.

I have been told by Hweig & Co. many times, "Be wary! Look under the words." So let us look under the words, under the event, under the incident. What was the purpose of this name game? On the surface it might seem sentimental, as we would call a good friend by a diminutive or nickname.

Look under the surface and there is nothing sentimental about it. It is a code. It could as well be a number. Why? Because a code word is easier to handle in their dossiers or their computers. Possibly it protects their work and records. It might even protect us from interference by other persons or actions.

But wait! Do we simply become a code word to them, depersonalized, anonymous?

Here is another pattern. Each contactee is led to believe, or they try awfully hard to make us believe, that we are some important personage from the past, born again into this life and time to accomplish some marvel. I wonder how many Nefertitis are living happily today in the United States?

There are so many Napoleons, Alexander the Greats, Catherines of Russia, and we probably couldn't count the Mary Magdalenes. I even had one woman pull me down close and whisper in my ear, "Don't tell anyone, but I am Jesus Christ!"

Are we truly a reincarnation, or regeneration of that person?

To find the purpose of this pattern we again have to look to the effect. As soon as a contactee is convinced, or even not convinced but just curious, he will dash off to the library and learn all he can about that particular personality. With all that study he is unconsciously absorbing into himself the traits, mannerisms, and beliefs of that personality, unconsciously *changing himself* into a more or less different person. Maybe this is a great benefit. A retiring person who has much to offer but is too timid to come forward, may be stimulated by a powerful *role model* to round out much needed areas of his own personality. Perhaps to the good - if he does not lose sight of the fact that no matter who he might have been in antiquity, he is today, in this lifetime, still Arthur Jones. Our mental hospitals accommodate those who forget.

Another pattern: Each contactee is told that he alone is *the chosen one,* chosen to save humankind and the world. Obviously each contactee has been chosen for his qualities and attributes which the peoples of the UFO's hope to bend to their uses, once they have reshaped him a little through various learning experiences. And who can foretell whose finger in the dike will indeed hold back a flood of disasters?

To be told, and to believe, that one is *the chosen one* can inspire and motivate beyond all normal endeavors. Perhaps these many persons working beyond their normal capacities and limitations are precisely what are needed to accomplish the final task the UFO planners aspire to have done.

For whose benefit? We can't know until we know what all those individual tasks are. *Contactees must be taken seriously,* not for their surface experiences, which can be bizarre and appear ridiculous beyond belief, but for the sake of the meaning that lies beneath all those patterns, the modus operandi of the *masterminds*.

Then there is the pattern of the useless gadgets contactees are inspired to create. Look under the gadget. Where is the pattern? Each struggling inventor has studied, researched, experimented and learned a whole new category of subjects: mechanics, physics, optics, or whatever. The result of all that high tension learning is not the gadget, but the learning itself, the disciplines of self-training, the establishments of good working habits. Perhaps valuable contacts have been made, even financial ones, and vital discoveries that have nothing to do with the intended and probably useless gadget. The pattern, the purpose of the planners has been the self-education of the contactee in fields he never would have thought of entering, but in which the planners thought he had some aptitude.

The final pattern for observation today is the wild goose chase. I am more than a little shy to mention this one, because I cannot recall all the times I have flown the friendly skies trying to put salt on the tail of some wild goose. So many miles, so much time - and *so much money!* It has been fun, an adventure, probably as much as a little old lady in tennis shoes could handle. It has not been profitable as far as bringing home that goose.

But then, let's look under the goose. Is there a pattern? Oh my, yes. No golden egg, but a pattern. Why, in the early beginnings, did they tell me to go to Virginia Beach and find out all I could on Atlantis in the Cayce Library? Why did they tell me to go to the Smithsonian to research the Sumerian civilization? Why, when we were planning a family vacation in Hawaii, did Hweig tell me to buy a very good camera and learn how to use it? "And please," he said, "Do not read the instruction manual as you do a book, from back to front. Please start at the beginning!"

Hweig said we would take important pictures in Hawaii, and insinuated it would be of UFO's on Maui. He was careful not to say this outright in so many words. Well, we did not. By a series of strange impulses, we landed on a beach in Kauai that was covered with rocks with strange markings on them. These were later identified as letters in the Ogam alphabet and the Hawaiian language, and referred to such things as the summer solstice, an eclipse, and a map of the Pleiades. This set me off into a study of symbols and epigraphy, ancient alphabets, just as the trip to Virginia Beach set me off on a study of Atlantis, and the trip to the Smithsonian sponsored a study of ancient civilizations.

So each wild goose chase accomplished something other than what I thought I was after. Each was meant to widen my experiences, my areas of study and research, to refine my knowledge. I gained a wider perspective of the world. I traveled to places I never would have gone, studied subjects I never would have noticed, and met delightful people I would have missed and never known.

Perhaps this is the best and most brief conclusion I can offer: that this whole lifetime affair has been a process of self-development through experiences, some of them very weird indeed, which seemingly have been imposed upon me.

"Not so," says Hweig. "You wanted to be able to help your fellow man. We simply have guided you to do so."

I will let him have the last word — he likes that. Says Hweig, "Now the great question, 'How dare we invade Earth minds to the extent we have?' Every mind we have in any way entered acquiesced to this use before that person appeared bodily on Earth. Reincarnation is a fact. Pre-birth induction into the ranks of our workers is an absolute necessity before we can engage that person, in his present Earth life, in our purposes." And now, for both of us - Thank you.[2]

---

[2] Dated 1988

CHAPTER SIX

Earth and Human Rejuvenation

AMORTO

Delivered at 10th Rocky Mountain UFO Conference[1]

We began our interference into your life many years ago and for a specific purpose. That purpose is now at hand and you will follow our instructions exactly! (Amorto's instructions to Ida were to take down this dictation.)

The first conference held in May 1980, was the beginning of a ten-year period of doubt and questioning.

At that time we delivered through Ida and others an outline of our general purpose in coming into your world and into your notice.

We are but one of many factions of Instructors who come from many alien sources. OUR particular purpose was to awaken an interest in psychic phenomena and the science of psychic development among your people. We have worked industriously at this for ten years and have seen the interest in all related topics as would fit under the New Age banner. We do not take credit for these developments. You, the individual contactees have done that, but we have been the awakeners to the veracity of such studies and we have propelled the manners in which many studies have been carried out.

Our precise course has been varied, and never in a straight line, always in circumlocutions and round about ways. You have all com-

---

[1] Laramie, Wyoming, USA; 1989.

plained many times that we seem devious and not always trust-
worthy, but over the course of years many of you have come to
understand that there was a reasonable purpose and a truth to
what we were saying, and for the various actions we were pro-
moting you to undertake.

Henceforth our instruction will be open and direct to those
of you who are willing to go along, a short time more, with us.

At the first conference we stated that one of our main purposes was to help in the reconstruction of the Earth and the evolution of Man. Many of you can attest that the activities you
have undertaken under our guidance and coercion have been
along these paths.

The reconstruction or rejuvenation of Earth is a gigantic
task but good steps are being made daily in that direction.

Not many of you have been in the area of Gas Hills, Wyoming. Go, if you wish to see miles and miles and miles of man-
made mountains, waste material from uranium mining. It is a
shock to the sight! Yet, a project is even now being discussed to
pour back as much as possible of this material into the holes from
which it came. This is but a local example of earth rejuvenation,
which will be seen more and more as the year progresses. People
are awakened to the need to repair the damages to nature that
have been so thoughtlessly wrought over the past 50-75 years.
You can read more statistics and examples in the daily news. It is
happening. And behind these happenings, working away silently
and unsung, are many of our contactees, quietly undertaking the
tasks that have been assigned to them.

Our second larger purpose to aid in the evolution of Humanity is through his psychic and spiritual awakenings and development, and we see a proliferation of books, workshops, other
aids and sources of instruction which are helping in these developments. Behind much of what you call the New Age activities
you will find a contactee or two patiently drudging away at his
task as we assigned it. Our workers do not announce themselves!
Many, we hope, will DARE to do so in the future.

One more reference to the 1980 UFO Contactee conference here at Laramie- -our instructor, whom you know as
Hweig, channeled the following message through Ida:

Changes are coming. Earth changes, as you know. Not to the point of utter catastrophe, as some have predicted, but like Mt. St. Helens as an example, there will be more of these local destructions all over the world. Earthquakes, tidal waves, other changes. There are going to be changes in political structures, in social structures that come on so fast! These institutions are going to crumble from within. It will not be outer war; it will be the inner harvest of their own misdeed. This seems to be coming into focus faster than we had believed possible. People must be strong. They will see something they have believed in all their lives crumble. They must understand that this is only the removal of the old before the building of the new. The old is crumbling from its own activities. There will be such a state of shock! The new must be brought from a stronger, perhaps wiser source, not necessarily US but through us from wiser people. I speak for worldwide.

And has any of this as given by Hweig in 1980 come to pass? Briefly consider the political changes and shortcomings revealed in our governing bodies. From Watergate to the Iran Contra affair surely confidence in your political structures has been thoroughly shaken. How many congressmen and others of high rank have left office in something less than ideal circumstances? Changes are taking place. The old is crumbling from within. But the new will build upon the ashes. In the financial world we have seen such scandals as the insider trading on Wall Street, and the shock of the failure of so many Savings and Loan and the largest banks. We have no time to go into detail here, but your daily papers will do it for you.

These are only foreshocks. Bigger, newer faster ones are yet to come. But then comes the reconstruction and that is where Our Instructors and the contactees have been trained to each do a part, large or small. They wait, many not realizing what the training and what the waiting are for. Those of you who are awakened contactees know precisely what I mean.

Now I have used up all of Ida's time, but I thank her, and all of you for listening.

Amorto
Head Instructor

CHAPTER SEVEN

Life with My Live-in Time Traveler

IDA M. KANNENBERG

In the beginning of our association Hweig managed to terrify me with his explanations of who he was and what he was doing and what he intended to do. I was most fearful that my mind was going to be taken over by an alien personality, that I would be possessed by another entity, and that I, myself, would be forever banished from this earth! I was not agreeable to that!

After more than eight years of this mental telepathic constant contact, I feel I am very much myself, even more so, for I know myself so much better. I have had to face up to myself. And Hweig is still only Hweig, a rascal, though an endearing one.

Believe me, this Hweig:Ida or Ida:Hweig collaboration and understanding has been reached with a great many battles between us, a great deal of stomping and yelling on my part, and a great many sighs and apologies on his.

People, curious, have been asking me many questions. What does it feel like to have someone talking inside of your head? Is Hweig always there? Does he give you answers to your problems? Does he prophesy the future? Does he ever interrupt when you are talking to others? Can he converse with you right now? How about privacy, is he always listening in and observing? Does he always know what you are thinking? Who is he anyway? Is he a person like us?

And so on. These questions are so often repeated I thought Hweig and I could answer some of them by this means.

What is it like to have a telepathic live-in companion who always seems to know everything I do and think? Well, sometimes it is sheer aggravation; I am married! And sometimes it is absolutely hilarious!

To myself, one of the biggest questions has always been: Why is Hweig a constant companion? Is he a monitor only? Why do the UFO personalities (whom he claims to represent) possibly care what I say and do every minute? I am not anyone. Why is my daily routine of such importance to them? Why did Hweig so entrench himself in my mind and in my life that I cannot dislodge him, no matter what I do? I have begged, pleaded, wept, screamed, but after reaching many compromises he is still with me.

Hweig has put me through some very painful processes, but he declares they were necessary in order that he learn my levels of tolerance and modes of reaction so that the best possible use might be made of my peculiar talents and abilities. Certain limitations had to be overcome, or at least ameliorated. And when I cuss him out from time to time I am only letting him know the limits of my compliance.

Eventually I told Hweig, "If you are really real, and a human being like us, and I should ever meet you, I am going to march right up to you and poke you in the nose for all the mischief you have given me."

He said, "If you do, I will turn you over my knee and spank you!"

To specify, here is one incident with my live-in companion I found amusing and exasperating at the same time.

Hweig had been nagging and pushing me to get some writing done and I had been bending over a hot typewriter for weeks, even months. I had been doing nothing except eating and sleeping and typing all without noticing that I was gaining weight. I began to have fierce pains along and between my shoulder blades, which I thought was from typing so much. One day I woke up to the truth! My bras were too tight. Believe me that can cause a real backache.

So I said to my mother, "I am going to walk over to the mall and buy some new bras. I need a size larger."

As I started down the road Hweig said," You will need two sizes larger."

I said, "I do not! I know what size clothes I wear!"

"You'd better get two sizes," said Hweig.

We argued all the way to the store. I picked out some bras I thought would do, arguing with Hweig all the while. When I took them up to the counter, a lady was checking out, so I had time to read a little sign:

"No lingerie may be returned after leaving the store." "You'd better try them on," said Hweig.

I gave a great exasperated sigh and said, "All right! Just to keep you happy I will!

And do you know what? He was right. I did need two sizes larger. But how did Hweig know that?

This was very puzzling. What was the extent of his prying into my life and actions? More troubling than that, what was his purpose in doing so?

I began to act like a paranoid cat watching a mouse hole. At the slightest sign of activity on his part, I pounced. I weighed and measured and analyzed and worried over every word he uttered, the way he uttered it, the time and place and conditions under which he uttered it, and counted every sigh, every laugh. I tried to detect his emotions beyond his words. Was he a little angry? Was he impatient? What was the reason behind what he said?

In all my cat and mouse surveillance I have learned how very human his emotions are. He is quite softhearted, very patient, gentle, considerate, a great tease, and his jokes are often on the ribald side. Sometimes he puts his foot in his mouth and then is cut off quickly.

"Oh-oh," he will say, "I'm not supposed to reveal that!" We have worked together for so long that his emotions will often leak over into mine. I will be very sad or euphoric or even come close to tears when I have no reason for doing so. I will say, "What's wrong, Hweig? Something is happening?"

And he will answer, "A plan has been cancelled." Or, "I've been given the go-ahead on a pet project." Or, "A dear friend is leaving us."

So I find my emotions can be affected by his. Talk about a Live-in companion, how close can you get?

When there are unhappy days in my personal life and I am feeling most disconsolate, I can feel a warmth gather around me, and Hweig will say, "Don't worry, Ida. Don't cry. Everything will work out right. It will be fine."

I take this, not so much as a promise, but as consolation offered by a dear friend.

Often Hweig has said, "I can see through your eyes and hear through your ears." I could not imagine how this could be accomplished. Direct questions never brought satisfactory answers. However, I do take showers with my eyes shut.

How could he see through my eyes and hear through my ears? Under hypnosis it was revealed there had been a UFO encounter many years ago at which time technological implants had been made. Consciously I mainly remember seeing a blazing red object come in over the desert at midnight. Bit by bit in these later years other remembrances are coming to mind.

Does such an implant sound implausible? Not when we read in the science magazines about brain implants in monkeys. Such a short step to audio-visual implants in humans.

With such mechanical devices that allow this, plus psychic abilities that permit further mind invasion and control, an alien, or an Earth, civilization could conduct any kind of surveillance, and their subject would have no defense against it, just as I have no defense against Hweig's constant surveillance.

The "aliens" can do this now. How long before Earth science can do the same? Or can they do it now? Can the "aliens" be Earthians?

I am not trying to scare talk. I am trying to relate what has been done to me by persons who seem compassionate and responsible. Can this be done in the near future by others who may not be as compassionate and responsible? Indeed, they could be utterly reprehensible! It is time to study what this kind of mind control, life control, is all about. The first place of information should be those contactees who have experienced it.

Hweig is very careful not to cause me any embarrassment. Except for one thing.

When he gives out with a hearty laugh, I laugh too. I do not intend to laugh. I do not want to laugh. I don't see anything to laugh about. But HE does and I laugh, and in a manner and to a degree that is not mine. "I am only trying to cheer you up," he says. "I do not like to see you despondent."

Hweig is an enormous tease. I suppose it does get boring and tedious always listening in to me 24 hours a day, though sometimes he takes a vacation for a week or so and someone else monitors. I try to tease Hweig back. The only trouble is he always knows what I am thinking as soon as I know it myself. Therefore it is very difficult to play any kind of joke on him. I managed it just once.

I was looking for a special skillet in the pantry and talking all the while, interiorly of course, and so rapidly that for once Hweig did not keep up with my thinking.

I said, "Not that skillet, it is too large, and that one is too small, that one is for square eggs, ah, this one is just right."

Back came a quizzical little query, "Square eggs? I don't think I ever heard about square eggs!"

I doubled over laughing to think I had really had the better of him, just once. A long time later he played a little joke on me, and said, "That is to get even for the square eggs. I never will live that down!"

Now doesn't that sound like a very human person, one not connected with my own sub-conscious?

I have included these little anecdotes here to point out a very important fact. Such incidents prove, to my own satisfaction at least, that Hweig is not an alter ego, my own subconscious, nor a tulpa. He is a very physical human being, quite separate from me, and very much like us.

There are several things I can do to drive Hweig up the wall. If I sneeze, or forget and whistle, he will say, "Please warn me when you are going to do that. A sneeze sounds like thunder and a whistle pierces my eardrums like a dagger."

Of course there is the problem that everything I can see, he can also; not only Hweig, but his immediate "crew". Since their observation is through technological implants the whole scene can be played upon a screen, like our television, so Hweig says. I have tried to explain this to people, but no one takes me seriously except my dear sister.

"You mean he can see what I am doing right now?" she asked.

"If I look at you," I answered. "And that is why simple situations can become rather delicate."

Another reason why I believe Hweig cannot be part of my own personality is our difference in food tastes. I used to order extra dill pickles with a hamburger until Hweig came into my life. Now I cannot eat pickles, or peanut butter, or bananas. Hweig calls bananas "monkey food". He says he cannot tolerate sour food of any kind, and that peanut butter stuck in his throat though he liked the taste. I advised him to eat it with honey or jelly. Later he said honey was fine and he was eating it with gusto. I was too.

As far as his personal appearance, I cannot know. I am supposed to have seen him many years ago when I was taken aboard a UFO, but I do not remember this consciously, and even under hypnosis I cannot visualize him.

Once in the earlier days when I was still completely uncertain about Hweig I said, "I wish you were really real so I could call you up on the telephone and talk to you."

He about bounced me out of my chair laughing. "How could you possibly talk to me any better than you are right now?"

"You would seem more real. This is too much like talking to myself." I explained.

So Hweig declares he is a very real person, physically human, totally dissociated from me, and that someday we will meet. Someday. Somewhere.

He describes himself as having dark blond hair, eyes "as blue as the skies", and like the Mayan gods of old he has four digits on each hand.

Hweig never becomes overtly angry or yells at me. Except once. He was trying to tell me something important to him, and just to tease I kept talking, talking, talking until he yelled, "Ida, shut up!" Have you ever had anyone yell at you inside of your own head? Of course he apologized later, but I told him I had yelled "shut up" at him so many times he could have that one for free.

One troubling question: how does he impel me to do certain things without speaking to me? Only afterward do I suspect he has somehow impelled the action. Sometimes I will walk to a window and stand looking out, or I will go out on the deck, and then suddenly realize where I am, and think, "What am I doing here? I'm supposed to be washing the dishes."

"You are getting a shot of energy," says Hweig, but he will not explain further.

How does he inveigle me, without speaking, to be in a certain place at a certain time for something unexpected and usually wonderful to happen?

Once, one of his colleagues said one morning, "We have planned a nice surprise for you today. We hope you will be pleased."

After several very improbable coincidences I ran into friends I had not seen since the Laramie conference in 1980. They were just as startled as I was. They had not planned on being in that area at all that day.

I no longer wonder overmuch who Hweig really is. What difference does it make? What matters is the fact, that whoever he is, he is unmistakably here and influencing my life in minute detail, obviously guiding me toward a particular task he- -or they—want me to accomplish.

Or has it already been accomplished? The years with Hweig have been a period of self-development. I am much more self-confident, more out-going, more interested in a wider area of world problems. Perhaps this is my term paper, to bring to those who read the revelation of what it is like to have one's mind and life so invaded.

Somewhere along the line Hweig told me that he and his two colleagues, Amorto and Jamie, who also speak to me frequently, were members of a vast organization dedicated to the task of keeping mind control from becoming a fact right here on earth. He asked if I would be willing to become a member of that crusade and I said I would. Perhaps that is the reason I have been so relentlessly invaded by them, to reveal what can be done with a combination of technological and psychological and psychic powers. I AM THE AWFUL EXAMPLE!

Is it because the UFO personalities plan further invasions of this kind? Probably, though they have innumerable invasions of like kind and degree already under way. Or is it because such invasions as these are fast becoming possible from others- - perhaps from our own planetary sources?

Would an invasion from earth forces be handled with the same moral and ethical responsibility and codes of dignity that the UFO mind invasion has?

I have questioned Hweig about his ability to prophesy.

He said, "By probabilities only. I am NOT, I repeat, NOT superhuman. I can do only what you could do if you had an equal reservoir of information to draw from. We prophesy only by balancing potentials, by probabilities. Even so, we can be wrong; some things are not wholly predictable."

So many times I have been asked, "Why don't they give you something useful, like a cure for cancer?"

Hweig answers this, "What would you do, Ida, with such information? If I told you how to build and fly a UFO what could you do with that information? Would anyone listen to you on that subject? Do you have the capital and the knowledge to do the job yourself? I give you the information you can use. Those who can receive and use technological and scientific help ARE RECEIVING IT, though they may not have a live-in companion as you do. They receive in the manner in which they are able to, and given the information they are able to use."

I ask Hweig, "Why is there this influx of extraordinary help at this particular time? Why now?"

Hweig's answer: "At this time Humankind stands in the dead center of the crossroads of human endeavor. I do not mean anything so simplistic as a single crossroad, but a convergence of many, many roads, each seductive in itself. A compromise must be made and maintained if world civilizations are to endure. The compromise must react onto many levels of human activity. World government leaders are struggling to find compromises on a political level, but the everyday people of the world must find their own ways of compromise on an individual level, such as levels of personal beliefs, religious as well as many other kinds. The metaphysical cores, not the history, of all religions should be studied and the psychological needs that shaped those beliefs. Only on that level can compromise be found, and until it is the fires and fervor of war will continue to brutalize the human race.

That was the only commitment Hweig would make relative to religion. "We are not here to tamper with your beliefs," he said. "Only to find a compromise and understanding among them all, to find a set of humanistic values that all can tolerate and refer to."

Often he has warned me, "Do not let any information we give you become the basis for a cult or a religion. No cults! No religions!"

I ask Hweig, "Why has all of this come into focus right at this time?"

"For the first time in the course of this round of civilization world-wide communication has brought all the differences of belief and activities into a coherent area of observation. Patiently many individual researchers in many lines have been digging into their specific studies. With the advent of computer technology all of those separate researches can now be brought under one roof, so to speak. They can be analyzed and studied on a comparative basis. Religion, for example, must be compared to mathematics. Does that sound silly? It is salvation! Archeology must be studied in relation to electro-magnetic waves. Only with computers can such comparative studies be adequately carried out. And they will be. This is the direction in which you are being guided, all contactees are, and in the sharing and comparing of information which can then become a common basis of understanding."

Another direct question, "Am I being mind-controlled?" Hweig's answer, "Only to the extent necessary to impel you into those studies and activities that will further our purpose, to have you gain information to share and compare with others. This in turn will further your own purpose to contribute to the health and continuance of your own civilization."

I ask, "Who gives you the right to thus invade my privacy, my mind?"

"You do," he said, "By the fervor of your desire to help your own people. You asked to be guided to a way to be of use, of help. This is a response to your own request. You put it into words and we answered. How else do you expect it could happen?"

I assume he is telling me no one is going to perform a miracle for us. If we want to save or help our civilization we are going to have to bestir ourselves to the task. We will have guidance, and information will be brought to our attention; the action- -or inaction—is ours alone.

The first necessary action is data analysis and comparison. The compiling is already done. Every contactee is a gold mine of source material. We must learn how to extract and use it.

We outline these needs by asking, "Who, where, what, how and why?"

First, Who? That would be trained workers, scientists, students competent to obtain and utilize information.

Second, Where? In a research center with adequate facilities.

Third, What? To study contactees who are willing to divulge their information and to be studied themselves in their interaction with the UFO connection.

Fourth, How? By devising a data code comprehensive enough to cover ALL of the forthcoming material. This can be modified and extended as the work continues.

Fifth, Why? To define specific plans of action, the manner and means of using that material once the information is obtained.

Another question I ask Hweig: "Why is all this information given to us in this peculiar fashion? Why all the mystery and camouflage?"

His answer: "UFO personalities and their activities are only one fashion in which information is being given. The UFO personalities can handle the type that leads to psychical research and psychological research through scientific disciplines. Technological, medical, and other scientific information and help is being disseminated by other means."

I know that all over the world there are others who are experiencing the same phenomena as I, a constant telepathic contact with other entities all of whom claim to be of the UFO fraternity. Although they may introduce themselves as several varieties of being, they are all UFO connected.

It is my belief we are the vanguard of an experiment that will, in the future, be expanded to hundreds and thousands more of earth's inhabitants.

It is important, therefore, that we begin to compare notes on these very personal experiences and to try to discover that big important question, "Where is all of this leading us?

This is a far more profitable question than, "Are UFOs going to invade earth at some future date?"

We are already invaded. The UFO personalities are already here, in our minds in these telepathic contacts.

While others tell us we are crazy, or fooled by our own subconscious or experiencing a split personality, or some other aberration the UFO people are blithely taking advantage of all this time to dig in and establish their territory in our minds.

There are tremendously ticklish questions here to be answered, but without profound research, such questions cannot be answered.

While we older folk have been the experimental, the trial and error stage, of the UFO mind invasion, our young people will be next. With their thinking powers numbed by constant frenetic entertainments, aided and abetted for some by alcohol or drugs, their minds could become so benumbed, bemused, and bewildered that any invasion of mind, alien or Earthian, would be a cinch.

There comes a time when one individual and his immediate associates cannot provide all the capital and energy and facilities needed to conduct and complete complicated and adequate studies.

It takes the backing and cooperation and support of those willing and able to devote their assets, both monetary and intellectual, to the task.

Believe me, our world governments are not without some recognition of the problem, but they do not go to the source of the information they need, the contactees, and the contactees' contactors. This is where the concepts and ideas and beliefs are being entrenched that will ultimately expose the meaning and the purpose of the whole UFO event.

Fellow contactees, I salute you! You are more important than you think![1]

---

[1] Dated 1981

CHAPTER EIGHT

The Great Contactee Hoax

IDA M. KANNENBERG

In the beginning of my experience with the self-called UFO personalities, I was completely skeptical of their reality and their validity. Were they indeed who they said they were? Did they intend what they pretended to intend? After years of working with them (at least that is how they refer to what I have been doing) I am still skeptical, and still unable to verify one word of anything they have told me except by its plausibility in some instances, and by its corroboration with other contactees' stories in other instances, and very rarely, by something happening as it had been promised, seemingly beyond simple coincidence.

We, who have had these personal experiences, are as baffled and confused now as when we began, some of us many years ago, some more recently. Nothing seems to make much sense, nor does it cohere into any understandable story. What is said one day is contradicted the next. Various parts of a single story seemingly contradict other parts. The total result is not only to confuse us, the contactees, but to render our stories absurd and usually condemned as false.

From my own personal experience I know that if there is any falsity in what I have related at any time the falsity did not originate with myself, but was perpetrated upon me. I, the contactee, am the victim of the hoax.

For many months I have been making notes, comparing stories of many contactees, trying to ascertain some reasonable reason for the confusion which has been given. Obviously, those who perpetrate the hoax do not want the various contactees to corroborate each other to any degree, else why the many contradicting stories? Are all these stories simply the psychosis and neurosis of the contactees working themselves out into the consciousness? If so, why are they doing so at this particular time and in such a similar manner? Since the stories hold so little in common, it must be the manner in which they are invented conceals the underlying principle that will cohere all UFO experiences into an understandable purpose, that is, the purpose of the UFO personalities in presenting these experiences.

Why has the scenario of each individual contactee experience been worked out, given, directed in the manner in which it has? And do all of these scenarios have any common basis?

Once the word "scenario" suggested itself to me, the next word was "drama" and then the question, "What is the purpose or the main result within the drama itself?"

To determine my way in answering this question I studied the traditions of drama and dramatic technique. The answer to my question was: One main objective of all good dramatic technique is CHARACTER DEVELOPMENT. Could that be the purpose of the UFO experience? If so, each contactee would, of course, be given the experience and told the story that was tailored to fit his personality, as it was, and the character he was destined to become. Therefore, each scenario would differ in its superficial content.

But, it seemed, no sooner was the contactee brought to a certain place in his development, in his scenario, than a purely farcical or patently absurd element came into his progress. If the story of his experience as it was related at first was acceptable there came a time when it seemed obvious delusions, or hallucinations, or completely absurd behavior seemed to take command. Something would happen as though he were being sabotaged by some independent force or personality in such a manner that the entire story of his experience would appear as pure fabrication on his part, as though someone meant to erase the validity of it all. Was this an effort on the part of his "instructors" to keep his story, and the stories of others like him, from being compared and the truths known? Or was the interruption that of some conflicting element in opposition to the UFO instructors? Was it an effort to wean him from over-much dependence on his UFO advisors?

Or could we explain this behavior as simply irrationality on the part of the contactee, due to the sudden release from the binding constrictions of his UFO contact, and the need to keep up the excitement and adventure of the state he found himself in while "working" with them?

To be sure, the contactee himself was not always aware that he had still been working with the UFO personalities long after his initial contact. Again, his initial overt experience may not have been his truly initial contact. That might lie long in his past and not be consciously remembered.

So many questions . . . so many confusions. Certainly there was no quick and simplistic answer. But after many months, indeed years of effort, one fact stood out, proclaiming itself loud and clear: The greatest hoax was that perpetrated by the UFO personalities on the contactee. The contactee was VICTIM, probably as much of his own naiveté or willingness to be of service to his fellow humans as of the projected trickery of the UFO persons. These qualities, perhaps his best, were utilized by his captors, exploited by them, to further the ends they sought. And if those ends were for his own benefit in the long run, the manner in which they were achieved frequently shattered his former life.

Was this, too, done for his benefit, to free him from his current status of self-imposed crutches so that he could stand free and alone and firm within himself? Or was it to make him available for the further purposes of the UFO personalities?

Who wins and who loses? And what is won or lost by the Great Contactee Hoax?

If each contactee were asked in retrospect, "What do you feel you have gained by your UFO experience?" would the answer, in effect, be: "An extension and strengthening of my character, a refinement of personality, a firming up of my convictions, and the ability to stand on my own two feet without leaning on anyone"?

And then the next question would be: Character development for what purpose? Whose purpose? When will that purpose be known?

And so one question but leads into another. For each one answered several more pop into being. The purpose of this essay is to take these questions and follow them into various avenues of exploration, trying to find the reasonable and plausible purpose of the whole, the UFO contactee experience, and to explain, if possible, the reason behind the Great Contactee Hoax.

When the UFO people approach us in lonely and frightening ways, when they put us through terrifying experiences with no explanation except, "Forget it," when they give us sworn statements that turn out to be perfect lies, when they play hide and seek, "Now you see me, now you don't", I for one cannot accept them wholly and unquestioningly as compassionate benefactors, totally here for our good. While we may benefit, even greatly, from interacting with them, the final benefit could as well be their own. Too often they do not treat us as human equals but as retarded nincompoops!

Probably they are not forces of evil. What they do they do from their own viewpoint and in their eyes it is good. What I see from my viewpoint is too much trickery, too much camouflage, too much play-acting, and I find it unacceptable as the acts of brave and compassionate beings, but rather as acts of exploiters and self-seekers.

What then are the UFO scenarios telling us? What is the final effect of the contactee episode when the silvery instruments of fate fly away soughing softly into our minds, "Do not fear. We come as friends. Remember us and wait until we come again".

What seeds have been implanted in our minds that we unconsciously nurture and culture until they come again?

We will not begin this search with statistics, counting noses and neuroses of contactees, nor follow any of the usual procedures. We feel a whole new approach is needed.

Later it will be necessary to know how the experience is projected into the contactee's mind. Was it truly a physical event, a psychic manifestation, a technological result such as from a hologram?

Later we may try to ascertain if those "facts" given are true or false. But what is important right now is the purpose of the scenario and its effect upon the contactee and his entire "audience". This means the all-time effect as it reaches out into his future life; religious, political, social, economic. What happens to him, and what is the final or overall result of what happened? And more, what is the effect of that happening upon his personal audience?

For this we must interpret the facts of the event for their symbolic and allegorical content, not from the standpoint of true or false, but from the standpoint of what these facts might mean to the contactee involved.

For these factors to have vital significance, we must accept that the entire scenario was planned, prepared, projected upon a specific person at a specific time and place. Everything in the event was minutely planned, perhaps long before. Nothing was left to accident or chance; therefore it had to be planned upon the pre-knowledge of the contactee himself. "They seemed to know all about me." How many contactees have reported so?

The incidence of UFO contact with persons of non- impressive status is far more prevalent, evidently, than commonly realized. If all these folk were to come forward at once to relate their stories, there would not be enough qualified investigators to hear them. Someone, somewhere will have to lay down specific "rules of order" so that all stories may be investigated on an equal basis, using similar criteria, and exposing comparable data.

Is there, then, such a basis, perhaps an underlying theme running throughout all the varying scenarios of UFO contacts?

We have noticed the element of dramatic technique, the necessity of observing character development of each contactee, that each scenario seems tailored to fit each unique individual.

The outer form of each scenario is drastically different from each of the others, yet underlying the symbols and allegories the same exact purposeful drama will be found.

Symbol and allegory are "put over" or gotten across to the contactee by predominately psychic means, by enforced illusion and hallucinations, hypnotically induced, and by telepathic and sometimes verbal or oral communication, also engineered by hypnotic means. A smaller portion, however, is certainly actual physical event.

Underneath the surface scenario we look to find the basic theme, or themes, for these are a geometric conglomerate of theme, branching off into many relevant issues and purposes.

An effort must be made to devise a dictionary of reason behind the elements of the scenarios, and thus to decode the pattern of the myth

Why each contactee was told a specific detail was based on what he already was, and this element lays the contactee story open to suspect, as though it is something evolved from the recesses of his own subconscious. Not so, the detail was presented because somehow the UFO Planners are able to discover what lies in the subconscious or past life of the contactee, and to draw from his own resources the elements they need for his own individual "myth".

What factors do we need to know about each contactee so that we may translate the scenario of each according to one understandable pattern?

We must know such things as:

His physical data, age, etc.

His mental development, education and emotional state His ideas, beliefs, manner of solving problems and perhaps a great deal more.

In another writing a detailed outline of such research will be given.

When we know what each element of the scenario meant to him specifically, we will find that in all scenarios these specifics will repeat, and repeat, and repeat, until the many-avenued pattern of the underlying theme will be apparent. This does not mean the surface facts of his story; it means the decoded elements of his personal myth.

For the moment let us try to determine the method by which the scenarios were put together rather than analyze the contactee.

To do this we must first consider the manner in which each contactee was approached on his initial contact.

Where was he and what was he doing?

We will find in each instance he was engaged in a very usual, very typical task, or more probably, pastime. He was at leisure, or it was during a rest period or relaxed moment, or going to or from work, seldom at work itself. His mind at that moment was roving, musing, or perhaps half asleep. This relaxation, or lack of tension of mind, is an important factor.

Secondly, he had just previously been intensely concentrating on an unusually troublesome personal problem. This might have concerned his family, job, money, love life. A deep concentration for some extended period of time had preceded the moments of mind relaxation. This "set the emotional stage" of his inner resources to respond to an unusual event. His responsive chords were in sharp, good order, oiled and ready to go, but for the moment, relaxed.

At the moment of the contact, the contactee was brought to sudden sharp attention, a general tension of all physical, mental, emotional, psychological responses. It was an instantaneous response from leisure to snap attention, all systems GO. This snap response is the second vital factor.

A.   Relaxation after prolonged tension

B.   Snap response to contact stimuli

The next element to consider was the time the contact took place, and what that particular time meant to the contactee. Was it midnight, the witching hour? Was it dawn, the time of new beginnings? Was it late afternoon, the time of approaching rest? Was it Sunday morning, the time of worship? This seemingly insignificant factor is the third most vital to our analysis. It sets the subconscious meaning of the event to the contactee:

C.   The time of the event.

The next factor to consider is that of the manner in which the contactee habitually solved his problems. It was certainly known beforehand and the knowledge accommodated in the planning. Would the contactee scream and run, remain calm and curious, become aggressive, or observe and think?

D.   Probable contactee response

E.   For this we may consider the specific need of the contactee for other human participation in his life. Was he in dire need of a confidant, an advisor, an authority figure, a religious entity, someone to care for, a comrade? Here we are getting deep into the needs and longings of the contactee.

We cannot always deduce the precise answers to these questions for each individual, but here and there throughout the telling of his story evidences of the answers will peep through.

F.   Perhaps the next most vital factor underlying each scenario is attitude of the contactee to outer interference in his life. Would he be receptive to advice, steering, prompting, and inspirations? Is his mind open to suggestions?

G.   Relative to this would be the rigidity of his preconceived ideas. Has he an open mind? Is he willing seriously and amiably to consider new ideas? Has his mind been congealed into traditional patterns of belief? Has his education placed him in a position of rigidity of discipline; scientific, academic, theological or otherwise that offers him no opportunity for New Thought? Is his mind malleable to reason? (Though that reason may be temporarily obscured behind a facade of mystery.)

H.   Can the contactee be counted on to carry out a task, a plan, a program, an opportunity to a final conclusion, or will he be inclined to quit at the first obstacle?

Maybe we should stop here for a moment and think of the contactees who have been prominently analyzed for us in various publications. Each of us will have a few favorites. Compare these with our eight projected factors of scenario plan. Regardless of the contactee's diversity of background, education, personality, does not a composite picture begin to emerge? This is only the veneer of the scenario; the various levels of its meaning will provide more and more elements for "compositing" a potential or actual contactee.

Then comes the all-vital question: Is this contactee one who would be willing to work relentlessly for the good of his fellow humans regardless of sacrifice, harassment, and cost? This is the major unifying factor of all scenario design. Without an affirmative answer in some degree to this question there is no scenario, no myth, no dramatic story, no contact, and thus, no contactees!

While this reveals purpose behind the event of contact, we must remain undecided for the moment as for whom that benefit will attain. The benefit to the fellow human of the contactee, or those who planned the event, or both, or all? We must not overleap caution with desire.

Beyond skepticism, however, we must consider fact. What did happen, what was felt, what was portrayed by the events experienced by the contactee?

If our discussion seems pedestrian, or even tedious, careful picking will yield the results we are after: understanding.

The fact of the initial encounter, it's more or less shock, its aftermath, these further our approach to understanding the totality of the contactee experience.

In the initial encounter the contactee was made to realize his relationship to the UFO, its occupants if such were observed, and the expectation of himself relative to the event.

What did the contactee expect to receive as a result of the occurrence? Knowledge? Aid? Power? Self-fulfillment? How did he interpret the meaning or purpose or result of the event to his future? Was he fearful? Was he filled with joy, longing, aversion, disgust? Was he apprehensive of what others might say or think if he told his experience? His TOTAL emotional reaction was not only important to his future scenario, but was anticipated and planned for.

Did he report to authorities? Did he keep the experience totally to himself? Did he pursue research into allied phenomena? Clues to what was anticipated in his reaction are found in the information he acquired at the scene of the contact. He was primed at that time to react in certain ways typical of him.

Without the priming he might have had a choice of a half dozen typical reactions. Reinforced by the priming, one reaction became dominant and was carried out as the Planners had anticipated.

One instrument of such priming might have been an object seen on or near the craft, if there were such observances in his initial point of contact. Did he see what he took to be a computer, or computers, or technological devices of an extremely sophisticated nature? This heavily reinforced his typical reaction of seeking scientific/technological explanations or advice. His experience was totally in line with his life and character, pre-planned to carry through on a line consistent with his own manner of thought. His choice of action was narrowed and reinforced. It was not distorted nor compelled. By such subtle means the Planners gained their objective, whatever it might be, while the contactee could feel he was acting with entirely free will, completely on his own.

This manner or method of the planners obtaining their ends must be called to mind frequently as we progress.

In short, something in the UFO experience reinforced the contactee's future activities, not in an entirely new direction, but in a renewal of a former objective or in the intensification and clarification of a current one. His life's goal and method of attainment was illuminated by the event, not by any directive he was given, but by something he saw. What was his outstanding visual impression? How does it relate to his life's goal?

We are speaking of his initial contact, and for some contactees this is still hidden from conscious knowledge.

This initial contact is Act 1, Scene 1 of our scenario, and it is in it we have found all of the necessary basic ingredients of drama: time, place, setting, the antagonist UFO, the protagonist contactee, his character and background and traits, and the individual story problem.

They use the ideas we already have to put across their message. Therefore, if the events magnify our religious or other beliefs, it does not necessarily mean the UFO personalities agree with these traditions or rules. They simply do not oppose our having them. Each to his own.

In each episode of the scenario they try to make us face ourselves, to make us learn something about ourselves, and at the same time, something about them.

Now to pursue another avenue of the purpose.

As in all good drama, it is all done for the sake of the audience; that is what it is all about. In this instance the contactee becomes part of the audience as well.

We find the total UFO audience in several places:

First, the contactee himself;

Second, his relatives, friends, confidants;

Third, those more professional researchers, investigators, to whom he relates his story; and

Fourth, the general public as, if, when they become aware of his tale.

What is the effect of the UFO experience story on the audience?

For the contactee: self-awareness and character development (or rarely, dissolution).

For friends: confidants: and awakening.

For researchers and professionals: facts to compare.

For the general public: a preparing, a making ready, a growing awareness of the overall situation, or a "softening up."

For all of this audience we see the general purpose of each contactee drama, and subsequently of all contactee scenarios, is a processing, a making ready. This is the reason why events are planned as though acts in a drama. This is why a contactee often feels the encounter is hazy and dreamlike, not quite real. It is real enough, but it is not reality, it is an allegory with facets often presented through symbology. The ultimate aim, the UFO persons would have us believe, is initiation into a vast organization dedicated to the betterment of humanity on Earth, a kind of recycling of man. They claim themselves as PART of that organization, the introductory and processing part. This does seem to be the WHOLE PURPOSE OF THE PRESENT STATE OF UFO ENCOUNTERS. The final purpose of the UFO personalities, and the PLANNERS behind them, may be something else again.

Now we must analyze the Architecture of that drama.

The basic architecture for the UFO drama is the general outline for scenarios used in UFO contacts. Specific blueprints will be given later.

The basic premise of the UFO drama can be divided into two elements, the situational premise which asks a question, and the solution premise which provides an answer (though it may be tentative to fact). The situational premise, then, would be the question, "How can the UFO personalities and their

Planners indoctrinate us with concepts and purposes compatible to their own?"

The solutional premise would indicate many encounters on different levels are needed to reveal their major secrets and purposes.

The theme of the drama would be secondary to the basic premises, more universal, not so specific to individuality, and would encompass something like: If you wish to be understood and accepted by someone, you must allow them to encounter you even though great fear and repudiation be created, and you must continue with encounters until your purpose is conclusively accepted or rejected.

The contactee is the *Character* of the scenario, and about him we must follow:

Past of contactee (character)

Present personality

Beliefs

Religious

Political

Social

Ethical

Moral

Responsibilities

Ambitions

Life's directions (contactee's viewpoint)

Story Progress:

Introduction

First contact known for such by contactee

All background contacts as revealed by hypnosis, dreams, recall

Development of work for UFO persons

Understanding evolved

Character evolves

Revelation to contactee of factors and concepts

Story Crisis:

Contactee is asked to choose:

To agree to collaborate with UFO personalities

To stop all contact, ask for full release

To compromise, to be an interested observer, but not actual worker

Story Climax:

The actual choosing

Story Outcome, conclusion:

The initiation into full collaboration

Complete release

Compromise situation

Each encounter of the UFO event must illuminate, for the entire audience, some understanding of the UFO Plan on many levels, and also advance character development or self- awareness of the contactee.

Major conflict throughout is based on character, what the contactee understands and is willing to do vs. what the UFO persons want or expect.

At the moment the encounter becomes known, overt action will be precipitated in the direction of reshaping the contactee's life program, if it has not already taken place from the subconscious pressures of an encounter not yet known.

The following changes will be found evident in varying degrees for each contactee:

Restructuring his life more productively on levels other than material

Taking up more creative activity, possibly an old ambition strongly revived

An attempt to re-find himself amid the welter of responsibilities he has conscientiously undertaken. (We will return to this in more detail).

To each contactee the foregoing is his own "drama" from his own viewpoint. It is imposed upon him by the UFO Planners, but is relevant to his own character and development. His encounter and his reaction is, after all, a very personal and subjective thing.

Character progresses and changes occur as the contactee becomes ever less fearful, less skeptical, and becomes more trusting, until his desire to help in the purposes of the UFO personalities overcomes his fear. At the same time he finds himself restructuring his life goals and purposes.

To find the overall purpose we have to base our architectural analysis on the UFO viewpoint, the Cause.

To analyze the various contactee stories we have to use the actual piecemeal material they contain, the Effect, and then to decide how they specifically relate to the overall Cause or purpose. That specific analysis reveals the many layers of purposes in the UFO scenario or processing event. It gives us the blueprint by which they were constructed into the form demanded by the architectural plan.

Since we are more concerned for the health, happiness, and welfare of the contactee than we are that of the UFO personalities, we will devise our study from his viewpoint of being an actor in a scenario devised for and imposed upon him. Though we had first to find and understand the architectural plan, the Cause, before we could even begin to recognize the edifices that are being built all over the world - the constructs that come into being in response to that plan. The individual contactee, their edifices, the scenario in which they play, none of it makes any sense whatever until the Great Drama, the Architectural Plan, the Cause is evident, the Purpose of the UFO Planners and Processors. The immediate purpose is obviously to find instruments for their use, collaborators, but to know surely their final purpose we have to observe to what use these "edifices and constructs" can be put. Do they indeed aid in the rejuvenation of Humankind and the Earth?

In our struggles to understand the UFO purposes we seek Cause; to understand the Contactee stories we seek Effect. This is somewhat like trying to walk down both sides of the street at the same time. The best we can do is stagger back and forth between them, and incidentally cross the median ever so often.

In the analysis of the encounter:

The event can be factual, straight presentation, a physical event

It can be illusory, equally valid

It can be symbolic or allegorical; must be interpreted

We determine contactee character by:

His reactions

His expressed thoughts and feelings

We determine crisis by:

His mounting emotional response

His need for decision

We determine climax by:

His decisive action

We determine conclusion by:

The result of that action

The UFO personalities initiate the encounter or action.

The need for response and action is imposed on the contactee by the purposes of the UFO persons, but is relative to his own character and development.

Ideally, the contactee progresses in his reactions and development as he becomes less skeptical and fearful, and becomes more trusting and willing to collaborate, until his desire to help overcomes his skepticism and fear.

The last big question in the contactee's mind, the one leading to crisis (his need to choose) and leading to the scenario climax, is the question, "Are these personages who ask me to help them working for the benefit of Earth, or am I betraying my own people?"

When the contactee has reached the point of almost acquiescence, when he feels he accepts what the UFO people are saying, "We are here to benefit humankind," and he feels almost won over, almost ready to sign on, there comes the last terrible fear: ARE THEY TRULY HERE TO HELP US OR AM I GIVING MYSELF INTO THE HANDS OF MALEVOLENCE AND DISASTER?

All of his wariness and skepticism and fear have come together in one great question, "Am I betraying my own people?"

To come to the point of decision he MUST HAVE additional information, clues, and revelations.

This is the moment of truth, when he must be helped to find an answer to this all-important question.

Where does he find it? If he cannot wholly accept the word of the UFO people themselves, where can he find the answer? Through study in books, magazines, correspondence with others, professional advice; through any kind of communication that gives him a broader spectrum of information. For this there must be publicity of other contacts, analyzed and presented on a rational basis.

So far we have ascertained each contactee scenario is a given "myth" based upon what he is, but done for the sake of a general processing of those who come into contact with his story, as well as for himself.

Let us consider, then, how his story is constructed, the architecture, the blueprint, and the building blocks.

Each individual contactee story or scenario or myth follows the same specific architectural form and is constructed from the same kinds of basic material.

The scenario facade is put together through such elements as the following:

Sighting of a UFO

Sighting of UFO occupants

Questioning by UFO occupants Visit to the craft

Examination or physical interaction

Journey to other places

Information, explanations, demonstrations

Instructions, advice, message

Continued or later contacts

Visual recall

Mental recall

Emotional or psychological recall

Recall through hypnosis

Throughout the world there must be thousands of UFO contact reports, adequately analyzing and recording the data of the total scenario. This is a first necessary step, but in itself, superficial.

The blueprint of each individual story or scenario or myth reveals the inner structure of the drama behind the architectural facade. In its design it reveals the strengths and tensions and forces that create the form. We can witness this blueprint only through the varied reactions of the contactee to the events. These reactions were purposely brought about by the UFO Planners.

We cannot, at this point, detect all the subtle building blocks of the drama, the meaning of the symbolic presentation of the individual myth, but in studying the blueprint we are coming one step closer to that aim.

Every contactee experience of any kind follows the same blueprint, some more completely, some very sketchily, but all experience can be correlated as either real or symbolic representations of the following effects:

I. Physical Effects Involved

A.   Feelings or tingling, vibrating, or as electrical current passing over outside of skin

B.   Pressures around top of head

C.   Movement within forehead area

D.   Muscle jerks anywhere over body

E.   Contraction of any muscular area

F.   Absence of usual pains

G.   Feelings of receiving unseen currents or rays

H.   Stretches when thinking seems "frozen" or head is "too tight to think"

I.   Movement within brain as though it is being "flipped over" or pressed together or squeezed

J.   Activity of muscles not sponsored by self

K.   Breathing becomes more and more shallow

L.   Extreme "hot flashes" while concentrating (reading or writing, or just thinking)

M.   Extended dryness of throat or nostrils

N.   Impelled laughter, or laugh movements of muscles when self is not laughing

O.   Impelled action when self does not know why

P.   Sudden feelings of dizziness, weakness, or nausea, for no known cause, brief and light.

II. Emotional Effects

A.   First feelings of fright at contact suddenly assuaged and feelings of friendliness to replace

B.   Overwhelming desire to know all about "them"

C.   Absolute belief in what they are telling — at least while they are telling it

D.   Feeling of meeting old friends

E.   Feeling of repeating an action done before

F.   Feeling of knowing what is to come in the immediate present

G.   Feeling the contact will endure, either be repeated or on going

H.   Feeling one has been waiting all his life for this

I.   Feeling of reaching self-fulfillment if one continues to cooperateJ.   Feeling of being useful to others, to the world

K.   Feeling of humbleness

L.   Feeling of impatience and drive

M. Desire to learn "everything in the world" immediately

N. Desire to be part of something "important" as well as useful

O. Concern over effort to understand experience as it is happening.

III. Mental Effects

A. Recognition of one's own inability to understand most of what is going on or being explained

B. Wonder why one is being given so much information that seems useless to him

C. Observation of physical features surrounding experience seem dreamlike or hazy, not quite hard reality. Footsteps don't sound, etc.

D. Wonder why one was chosen for this experience

E. Concentration on detail seems impossible, details won't "hold"

F. Underneath insistence, "This can't be real," even as it is happening

G. Beliefs "I understand" immediately swept away by additional information definitely   not understood

H. Comparison of factors of information seemingly contradictory

I. Absolute conviction one is being "used"

J. Necessary to retain customary self-control by effort

K. Inability to put two and two together decisively

L. Mental apprehension over one's stability.

IV. Psychological Effects

A. Conscious effort to retain control at all times

B. Time disorientation complete

C. Factors of experience become stressful which ordinarily would not be noticed

D. State of apprehension increases with time lapse

E. Control diminishes with time lapse

F. Concentrated effort to gain upper hand in situation

G. Later ego status must be re-evaluated completely

H. Compromise with situation to retain emotional and mental control

I. Surprising elements reduced to acceptance by traditional interpretations

J. Mock rewards seen for persuasions and repudiated

K. Choice made according to altruistic concepts

L. Pressures offered on emotional terms ignored

M. Reaction of contactee to experience becomes a matter of life involvement.

V. Intellectual Effects

Increased interest in:

A. Extension of interests in many dimensions of knowledge and understanding

B. Wider area of concern for others

C. Constant attention to matters of world involvement, political, social, economic, etc.

D. Aesthetic and artistic studies

E. Self-expression, creativeness

F. Design for new areas of creativity.

Building Blocks:

The true building blocks are the reasons why the contactee reacts as he does to the events, his subconscious and inner makeup, his conflicts and turmoils and distresses, and to find these we must interpret the symbol and allegory of the myth he has entered into and become part of.

The interpretations will be found in the cultural context of his background, even though it illuminated his personal stresses.

By his cultural background we mean to indicate the scientific, technological, religious "spirit of his era" as much as the more formal ideas of culture.

By this fact we see the event is not of his own pathological devising but is induced from outside him. It is an illusion or hallucination which may be physically induced by technological devices, such as holograms, or by psychic illusions through hypnotic mental or telepathic suggestion, or other induced psychic experiences such as an out-of-body experience, and, or mind travel.

In the contactee cultural background, all-inclusive, will be found those elements that are objectified as the building blocks of his story. We need, then, to discover these building blocks by asking, "What do these culturally defined elements mean to the inner person, and how do they bring forth, objectify, his inner questionings, desires, and needs?"

To emphasize: The specific symbols chosen for the illusory or actual events of each contactee's myth are not derived from the experiential content of his subconscious but from the general cultural symbolism of the society in which he exists. The blueprint symbols are cultural; the inner stresses, the building blocks, are personal and individual.

It was possibly expected that once the illusory event was brought to consciousness through recall, through dreams, or through hypnotic regression that the contactee would recognize the symbolism and allegory for its intent and come to some understanding. Most often he does not, and is left baffled and fearful by what should have been a revelatory experience. Sometimes this non-comprehension is because he remembers too soon, or hypnosis brings forth material before the background of understanding has been gained. Its time of emergence into consciousness was fore planned, but accidents, such as slippage of subconscious material during dreams or hypnosis, recall the material before the tools of understanding have been gained or developed.

Like the salt mill the little old lady threw into the sea because it would not stop grinding out the salt, so the UFO illusory or actual event may lie imbedded in the subconscious of the contactee constantly grinding out its effects totally undetected by the conscious self.

Perhaps we need most of all to understand the UFO presentations as a dramatic portrayal of a reality beyond our four (counting Time) dimensions, and to understand it as a psychological reality, and we must learn to interpret the contactee experience on that basis.

We have observed that: Drawing the contents of each well-planned and fore-planned scenario from the cultural symbols of the individual in space and time, the scenario ingredients were fitted into the context of the generalized scenario in whatever manner or mode the contactee could most comfortably confront and possibly accept.

The outcome of these scenarios has been to hoax the contactee, though it was probably not so intended. He, in turn, passes on the hoax to his public, for he has neither manner nor means by which to distinguish the literary inventions, the illusions and induced hallucinations from actual occurrences and reality.

The public, doubting, and not under the magical spell of the UFO personalities, cries "Hoax!" upon the contactee. Poor fellow! Caught between the UFO perpetration and the public, he stands in an agony of confusion and self-doubt, and takes a beating not rightfully his.

There are many types, levels, kinds of scenarios, but those most often used in a given cultural area and time, are, without doubt, the ones considered by the UFO Planners to be those most vital to their purpose at that time and place.

The type of scenario seems to change more with time than with place, indicating a progression of intent.

Roughly stated, in the mid '50s we had the scenario of recognition, conforming the ingredients to our supposed level of understanding and possible acceptance. In the 1960s it was the scenario of biological intervention. In the 1970s it was the scenario of initiation. In the 1980s the scenarios accent the self-awareness and character development of the contactee.

The Planners' intent must have been to use dramatic license for effect and reaction, not to delineate fact.

Perhaps we were expected to recognize the invention and to distinguish them from physical reality, but not all at once. By putting stops on the memory of the contactee until it was "time to remember" the Planners meant to protect from confusion and fear. In the meantime the subconscious remembers and shuffles up little extracts from time to time as directives of action, as guiding principles. To come to some terms of understanding the scenarios, we must forget trying to see straight factual physical meaning, and study the subconscious or conscious effect that was intended beyond the confusion and fear that was engendered.

- A journey to the moon or Mars or Jupiter or Clarion or Venus and other marvelous adventures can be the result of one or of several projections.

- An induced illusion (an event under hypnosis)

- An imposed visual hallucination (also under hypnosis)

- A technological display, such as our TV, scenes played upon a screen

- A hologram, three dimensional and active

- An out-of-body experience

Mind Travel

How, then, can we draw any conclusions from a contactee experience, answer any questions, or add to our information? Certainly not by a direct adding together of factors taken from contactee stories, if they are largely the result of imposed illusions and play-acting.

Only by viewing the event as just what it was meant to be - a scenario, in a play act, a drama full of symbolism and allegory, perhaps - and real or analyzable only on the level of dramatic purpose.

Any vision or pictorial illusion is meant to be symbolic of an idea, not a fact.

The reason for symbols is to implant them into our subconscious, in areas where word symbols do not hold. It is an area where we resonate pictorially, not verbally, and that is why the illusory experiences are always made known to us through pictorial symbols. If we have a verbal communication, it is no illusion but straight out fact. (An obvious deduction but useful to verbalize here).

To make our study valid in the case of illusory experience we must ask this, "Was the illusion or hallucination or vision planned step by step, or was a hallucinatory episode set into motion and let run according to the subconscious nature?"

If the first is true, then step-by-step analysis of the entire illusion is in order. If the second, then just the fact of an illusion occurring is all that must be considered in reference to that particular study.

Is the illusion planned and presented step by step?

Is the illusory situation self-perpetuated once begun?

The UFO experience is intended as a cultural or societal event as well as an individual subjective one. The individual is necessarily subjectively influenced. A UFO hallucinatory or illusory event can be weighed and measured, its significance grasped, only as a WHOLE event, as the blueprint, therefore it is planned as a whole situation with each building block carefully inserted, each contributing to the whole effect, each chosen for its cultural (not individual) symbology. It is this fact that makes a meaningful method of decoding possible.

The consistency of the symbols and building blocks, and the consistency of interpretation possible to the scenario, indicates the illusion was deliberately manufactured and the specific scenario, among a number of possible ones, was chosen to affect that particular contactee in a definite manner.

It was a deliberate, indeed self-evident, purposeful event and the purpose is supposed to become known in the proper time.

The story line from the viewpoint of the UFO Planners is to find characters who will be or have (1) potential of understanding, and (2) strength of will or determination or obstinacy to overcome fears and carry understanding to a final conclusion initiation into full collaboration with the UFO personalities.

Then they interact with each of their contactees to develop their strengths to the final conclusion.

If the UFO persons are able to gain a sustained attention of the contactee, they bolster their explanations of themselves with a great many emotional ploys. They make promises, they use endearments, they create emotional attachments. Anything they can say or do to keep the contactee paying attention! Possibly some of their ploys are 100% sincere. Possibly the degree of sincerity is somewhat less. They seem to feel the Cause is so vital, so beneficial that almost ANY MEANS TO AN END is justifiable and forgivable. On the basis of THAT contention, we find much to complain about in their activities!

In each contactee event, the Planners try to reveal or teach something.

Always they try to make us learn by giving an experience and in going through such experiences the contactee not only learns, he develops himself. He does not weakly memorize tables or verse. Even if the event is illusory, there is something in it that aids or directs his life development.

As the UFO persons try to teach, the contactee reacts or repudiates out of:

A.   Direct fear of the experience

B.   Confusion

C.   Skepticism

D.   Lack of understanding

E.   Desire not to be gullible

F.   Desire not to be used

G.   Fear of being "taken over"

H.   Desire not to bring harm to family, friends, and public

As the "story line" develops, the UFO persons gradually win over the contactee, who listens from:

A.   Curiosity

B.   Sees opportunity to better self

C.   Desire to be helpful, amiable

The two level purpose of the UFO Planners is seen in the progress of character or life development and the intended audience reaction.

It is not necessary to assume the result is all as perfect as the Planners had hoped.

The unpredictability of human nature renders the results equally unpredictable.

The many subtle powers of the Planners and their obvious prestudy of all probabilities reduces the margin of error and possibility of failure in their attempts to a minimum. But the contactee's freedom of action and free will can, and often does, throw a monkey wrench into the works anywhere along the way.

Many scenarios doubtless come to something less than a perfect conclusion from the viewpoint of the Planners. The contactee may come to repel their bright lures and promises, fearful of collaborating self into mental sheep-hood or of betraying "his own kind." Such conflicts are many and intensely agonized by the contactee.

The mental contactee further undergoes mental tortures, fearful and resentful of the "alien voices" which invade his mind. Under such circumstances there is no mental privacy whatever!

The UFO personalities struggle to gradually win over the contactee into full collaboration with them, to indoctrinate him with their concepts and purposes, without interfering with his preconceived ideas or beliefs, or allowing him to get out of hand into absurd misconceptions. Also, the contactee can kick over the traces, taking off into self-propelled misdirection.

He can also deny his experience if he becomes frightened of what appears to be ahead. To get himself out of it, to disconnect himself from any further association with UFOs, he can repudiate his own story, hoping this will "be an end of it". He may find his UFO involvement has brought him anything but Fame, Prosperity, and Happiness. To deny his own story may seem a small price to pay for peace of mind for himself and his family. He may wish only to escape further harassment from various sources.

As in all staged drama, there does come a crisis when the contactee must decide whether to accept and collaborate with the UFO persons or not, and climax when he makes a choice, and the conclusion which is the outcome of that choice.

The myth is all one, but it is encoded differently for each individual contactee, in symbols derived from his cultural background.

All of the scenarios, decoded, become one single story, the exact same for all.

By decoding each contactee story we can find the underlying purpose and intent of the UFO Planners, and perhaps even glimpse something of the organization behind it all.

To do this we must devise, and re-devise, and re-re- devise a code that we can tentatively believe represents factors of their intent. We are working "backwards" to find the base. Once that has been adequately well established we can ask a contactee, "If you had to picture or visualize your ideas, how would you represent the following?"

A. Peace

B. Spiritual understanding

C. Self-realization

D. "Salvation"

E. Aliens from another world

And then compare these answers or symbols with the tale he has told, his individual myth. The symbols should make the myth.

Each contactee was chosen by the Planners because he was of such a character and attitude that appeared useful to their purpose, whatever we might think that purpose to be.

Some of the specific traits which all contactees share, must have in common to a greater or lesser degree, are:

A. Desire to be helpful

B. Seeker of knowledge

C. Desire and willingness and patience to learn

D. A certain tenacity or obstinacy or downright stubbornness

E. Open-mindedness

He must also be reasonable enough to know fear. Only through fear can he become wary and cautious and analytical. Fear may take many forms and dimensions. Each element of fear conquered and laid to rest increases the strength and understanding of the contactee.

The encounter is planned at the precise moment the contactee is psychologically, mentally, emotionally, in condition. Those who try to make the contact may not succeed immediately, but they will change tactics and try again. And again and again.

A. The timing of the contact can be analyzed through the following checklist:

B. Contactee's strong involvement with another, or others, has come to a mental or emotional crisis.

C. Contactee is debating a large change in his personal life.

D. Contactee is irritably dissatisfied with his present life.

E.   Contactee is highly desirous of taking up a new or long discarded creative activity, such as writing, painting, photography, or some scientific or cultural pursuit.

F.   Contactee is mentally aware of need to reconstruct his life more productively on levels other than material gain.

G.   Contactee has been aware he needs to give more attention to himself. He feels he has lost SELF somewhere in his work for others. He feels such self-sacrifice can be carried too far; he owes responsibility to him SELF also.

In short, at the time of the encounter the contactee has been under some strain or worry revolving around his feeling of the need to make important changes in his life. It has come almost to the point of mental and emotional crisis.

To summarize our scenario elements up to this point:

The UFO personalities burst upon the contactee at a moment in his life when he is ready for a vital change. He may have had encounters before that time, but they are buried in the subconscious, he had not been aware of them.

The event of the contact is tailored to fit the contactee, whom the Planners have studied and know thoroughly well.

The main conflict the contactee encounters is that of his own character as he is forced to face it through the activities of the UFO personalities. His fear and confusion versus his desire to be helpful and desire for his own benefit are the basic conflicts.

The Planners must have inquired of themselves, "What kind of person would respond to our presentation of ourselves on many kinds and levels of encounter contacts?" Then they would search for persons of that character to respond to their presentations, and would try to develop them into persons of understanding and usefulness to themselves.

Therefore, all contactees have certain similar basic traits and all presentations (scenarios) have similar basic ingredients.

The first contacts, whether physical or through mental telepathy, or psychic induction, are for the specific purpose of preparing the contactee for self-awareness and development, and potential future collaboration with outer forces.

If the UFO personalities' presentation of their purpose is valid, then the contact events will result in:

A. Preparation of contactee's physical self to serve as future instrument of "in-put"

B. Preparation of contactee to adjust mental, psychological and emotional states to acceptance of a helpful role in the future

C. Preparation of contactee to invest life in pursuits useful to humankind

D. Preparation of contactee to engage in activities of artistic, aesthetic, creative nature

E. Preparation of contactee to work for spiritual realization

F. Preparation of contactee to observe and cherish all things of nature.

Thus it is through the contactee we will find the deeper more hidden purposes of UFO phenomena. This does not mean the personality of the contactee, though that also must be known, but more exactly, the relationship of the contactee to the entire drama of the coming of the UFOs! He is part of the total purpose, though he has an individual meaning as well.

We are trying to understand two levels of purposes at the same time, why the UFOs come to us at all, and why they so process the individual contactee. There are mysteries within mysteries, and purposes within purposes.

As a contactee, I have given a great deal of thought to the contactee's part.

How many times I have reached a point of recognition and said, "Ah, now, that is the truth! At last they are revealing something truly true." And as I go about on euphoric wings for a day or two, I come flat-faced against another question, "But if? Then why?"

I feel I am going through a maze, a labyrinth, and when I make a "right choice", take a right direction, I progress a little further and feel momentarily very free and boundless, only to smack up against another wall in short order. Once again I have to live and agonize and make a decision, and if my choice is "right" I again progress a little further.

As I perform certain acts or go through certain events prodded by my UFO captors, I am expressing the event in action. I am not verbalizing or talking about it or exhaling ideas. I am performing Reality. I am not doing lip service or only making promises I may or may not be able to keep later. I am doing. I am acting. I am performing my Self. I am collaborating in creating my Self.

Now it is necessary to interject a little dictation:

Myth and Mischief

HWEIG

Now, I, Hweig, will dictate, as you, Ida, have no way of knowing how to interpret these events and scenarios.

First, we must emphasize the necessity to read the following in its entirety, as we can give the total story only bit by bit, and later bits will clarify earlier bits that might discourage the reader if he were not forewarned. Therefore, please be patient, ride all the way through with us, then judge according to your own understanding.

About 80% of all UFO abductions and personal contacts are the result of hypnotically induced illusion and hallucination.

Those who perpetrate this hypnotic state and its seeming events are unseen but present within the room, car, or otherwise near the contactee. This unseen presence is often felt by sensitive persons and all of our contactees are MOST SENSITIVE as a pressure in the atmosphere immediately surrounding them. The presence is projected by technological means much beyond the powers of your own people at present. This indicates the presences are those alien to yourself, and not of your normal everyday earth person no matter how advanced in any science, technology, or psychic ability an earth person might be. The alien presence has powers far beyond anything you might dream of.

It is necessary for the alien presence to be in close proximity to the contactee. By close we mean VERY CLOSE, almost within touching distance.

This presence, being almost pure energy, need not be in any one particular form, but can attain any form or abstraction desired. Black and white pinwheels, balls of light, fireflies, revolving disks, any form may be utilized to come momentarily into the vision of the contactee. We call this a semi-corporeal form or semi-physical state. Or the presence can remain totally unseen, in the state that is similar to your out-of-body experience, though the essence of that presence is of a more powerful energy than the essence of your out-of-body state. However, this is the closest analogy we can find to describe this energy state.

It would frighten you spitless, as you say, Ida, to know how many times you have been surrounded by alien presences. The knowledge of their extent of control over you would further alarm. This goes for all contactees of similar events.

For this reason, the potential alarm, we conceal the facts just given and instead perpetrate an illusion of physical aliens who seemingly come into the contactee's presence, or bring the contactee into theirs, knowing you can accept and interact with physical beings in a less frightened and more objective manner. Yet we wish to get across the idea of VERY ALIEN personalities, therefore we do not offer the visualization of your own kind of form, even though many of us are precisely your kind of form.

To feel you were being contacted, and perhaps controlled, by unseen forces, would throw you into a panic, perhaps beyond acceptance, but to deal face to face with physical beings, no matter how alien, would eliminate some of that panic. At least that is our proposition, and this is why these illusory beings appear.

Not all contactees or abductees face illusory personages. A very few are quite physical and quite "real" as you term realness.

The illusory beings are the semi-corporeal selves of very real physical beings, who are at that moment existing in another area of being, and are quite busy doing something else physically, but are aware of what is happening in and to their semi-corporeal self.

This is certainly confusing. Let us recapitulate:

The unseen presences are there through technological means. They induce hypnotic illusion of abstract forms or hypnotically project the semi-corporeal forms. These latter are projections of real beings who are somewhere else physically at the time. They use projection "copies" because some time in the future these physical originals may find it necessary to interact with the contactees in a wholly physical manner. It would then seem to be an on-going experience.

Let us reiterate for clearness:

A corporeal, flesh and blood, person so projects himself in an unseen state through technological means that he enters into close presence of a contactee, or abductee, and is then able, through his own psychic power, to gain hypnotic control over that contactee when said contactee is in a relaxed state. If the personage were present in semi-corporeal or corporeal state he could control the situation equally well.

The contactee, being already in a relaxed state, is readily accessible to the hypnotic form of control.

What transpires thereafter is all illusory and hallucinatory, unless there is a need for physical interaction. In such a case the contactee can be conducted aboard a physical craft where the physical interaction occurs.

By physical interaction we do NOT include examinations per se, as these may be of either category, physical or illusory.

Why should it be necessary to go through so much physical effort when illusion will serve the purpose of the Planners just as well? The psychological reaction of the contactee and the mental and emotional results of his scenario, both to himself and to his audience, are what it is all about. If the same results can be obtained through hypnotically induced illusions and through actual physical action, then the illusion is chosen.

We are saying things backwards and forwards and inside out, so that, hopefully, no ambiguity remains.

The presence in the room, or car or wherever, with the contactee can be felt as an oppression, a "thickness in the air" as one contactee described it. The contactee begins to breathe in a shallower manner and to feel closed in, or caged, or captured, or unable to move.

The presence is the energy essence of a real corporeal being, who through technological devices, sends his energy self, in a state relative to the out-of-body state, to this place. Since he is not a psychic master he is not able to send his energy essence through his own psychic power but must depend on technological devices.

The energy essence encloses the WILL of the presence, who is elsewhere physically, but is linked through mind stuff to his energy essence and will.

And that human being is so restricted by moral and spiritual law he cannot, dare not, serve as an evil power. He carries out instructions received from higher natures, and by higher we mean more knowledgeable, more powerful, and more responsible. He is further instructed to use the most compassionate modes of interaction he can devise.

Non-understanding, haste, error of judgment, misreading of contactee's reactions, as well as many other factors can impose a task on the controller that he may be less than perfectly equipped to handle. Remember he is only another human being trying to do a very difficult job. He is working with persons as alien to himself as he is to them.

The presence of the controller is never seen by the contactee unless it is necessary to attract his attention, or to rivet his mind onto a single point. At such a time abstract designs or evasive objects, usually circular, are used. Other times the unseen presence can be felt or sensed by those most sensitive to such emanations of energy.

The condition and reaction of the contactee decides whether or not the presence is to be seen in any form or to remain unseen.

Many contactees have mentioned the "feel of an evil presence". The presence is NOT EVIL, but is part of the UNKNOWN and does take CONTROL for a few moments, and from the arising fear and apprehension the contactee interprets "evil".

The contactee response to the sense of being controlled is entirely according to his own nature and character. One resists and tries to struggle, one weeps or screams, one jeers, or even giggles. In the response, its kind and degree, the controller reads information it is necessary for him to know in order to continue into the future. The preliminary or initial scene is thus an act of getting acquainted, each measuring the other's potentials. Furthermore, the controller is just as much "on the spot" as the contactee, for him, too, is undergoing a training session and is being weighed and measured by his instructors.

From his own psychic and trained abilities the controller then conjures up the appearance of apparent personalities who seemingly take charge of the scene. These are appearances of substance, but not true corporeality. We refer to them as semi-corporeal. They are projections of real persons who are to be physically met in the continued scenario of the contactee.

If footsteps sound, temperatures change, and there are NO SUDDEN TRANSITIONS in the scene the event is entirely physical. If so, there are noises, odors, and the sense of touch as well as vision. Touch does not mean pain; pain is psychologically induced by the contactee through fear.

There can be a shifting of states, a moving in and out of states during the course of a single event, so a single event can be a very complicated affair. Each would have to be minutely inspected and analyzed to realize these changes. At this moment such a scrutiny is not important and would only obfuscate this recital.

Thus we see MIND TRAVEL as well as OUT OF BODY TRAVEL can be induced from outside the contactee.

It is within the framework that the building blocks of the individual myth are found. When we realize the changeable conditions of the contactee/abductee event, we can begin to understand why the scenario itself is so very difficult to grasp as reality. But in comprehending these varying and shifting states, the interpretation of the building blocks becomes much easier.

By symbolic event we do not mean symbols such as a cross indicates a good guy and an x a bad guy. We mean the contactee is put through an event that is NOT TRUE in its content, but its psychological effect symbolizes one or more of the following ideas. These events and the ideas they symbolize are the building blocks of the structure. Depending upon the cultural experience of the contactee the following ideas are presented in various manners:

I. Ideas presented in the Scenario of Recognition

- Of civilizations existing on other planets
- Of civilizations existing of fantastic technological achievements
- Of civilizations existing of tremendous scientific knowledge
- Of civilizations existing with people of various natures who have knowledge of all kinds: medical, artistic, cultural, etc.

II. Ideas presented in the Scenario of Biological Intervention

- Of cross breeding with "alien" races

- Of giving of ovum or sperm for breeding experiments
- Of implantation of sperm or fertile ova
- Of taking of cells for examination, experimentation, or for cloning
- Of interference with mental input, conscious recall, memory
- Of implantation of technological devices for later use.

III. Ideas presented in the Scenario of Initiation

- Of an unseen, secret organization of Good Will and Benefit
- Of inspirational aids to solve problems and difficulties
- Of secrets of the past to be found anew
- Of promotion of societal contacts leading to cooperative efforts
- Of monuments of good endeavors recorded in lost places
- Of destruction of powerful deterrents to human/earth collaboration.

IV. Ideas presented in the Scenario of

Self- Development and Self-Awareness

- Of offering new personal insights
- Of strengthening stabilizing beliefs
- Of offering new projects
- Of analyzing life-evaluations
- E. Of value of self-freedom
- F. Of support of person's intentions/ambitions.

There are many other scenarios and parts thereof, and these can each or all merge one into another. In order to analyze them at all we have to dissect the living form.

End of Hweig's Dictation

The overall effect of the contactee scenario is to make him face up to himself, to study, analyze, know himself, to concretize answers to questions he otherwise never would have asked himself.

As he expands his self-awareness, he expands himself into the world around him.

Once a UFO personality asked a contactee, "How can you know you are courageous if you have never faced danger?"

This could be extended into other attributes. How can you know you are honorable if you have never faced temptation?

In the final analysis of his self-awareness, the contactee proves to himself he can be stronger, or wiser, or more compassionate than he ever dreamed of himself being. In his final reaction to the UFO event, he magnifies himself.

In the UFO scenario or drama or myth we are made to stand face to face with ourselves and examine minutely all our fears and hopes and beliefs and joys and expectations and to measure them to the realness of our world.

We live through a hypothesis or illusion or dream and come in the end to the absolute understanding of our Selves.

I may not be a more highly evolved person because of my UFO contact, but I am an absolutely sure person of what I am and what I am not. If the UFO persons have not revealed themselves to us, they have certainly revealed us to ourselves.

In the various scenario events the UFO people put contactees through, we must make a choice before we can be told what the event means. The choice must be made so free of any pressure or involvement that we cannot even be told we are making a choice. Each right choice we make is a step in our self- development; each wrong choice is simply wasted time, unless we, ourselves, quit.

Where do the Planners derive the symbols they use?

From our books and stories, from our myths, legends, fairy tales, from TV and movies, from science fiction, from literature and poetry and fantasy, from the Arabian Nights, Tales of Scheherazade, and Sinbad the Sailor, —and maybe even Star Trek!

The Planners, the Dramatists, remain unseen and unknown. Those who are actually seen by the contactee are not those who have dictated nor imposed the event.

Where but in these fantasies from our own background could the Planners find the symbols we would recognize and react to and hopefully understand?

We take these borrowed literary inventions for real!

We must learn to decode the appearances, to learn what they are really saying, to interpret and translate. Then we shall find the whole scenario not so hard to understand, and understanding, to believe.

But why? Why come in this manner?

The UFO scenario is a learning process, and what we learn is ourselves. They do not come to teach us about themselves. The facade of the story is the great pretense: the playacting, the drama, the Hoax.

Behind the facade lies the reality of the UFOs in themselves, their inner meaning, and their purpose in coming to us at all.

"To aid in the rejuvenation of Earth and the future evolution of Man". So they have said.

Possibly.

But could it not have been done differently?

Probably not.

Like children our attention and cooperation must be caught and held.

"This hurts me more than it does you." And "I do this for your own good."

Do we not use such alibis to our own children? Do we not tell them all sorts of fairy tales and fantasies and myths and expose them to the total unreality of TV cartoons?

Could they not be more gentle?

As they have surveyed our world do they not see wars tearing the earth apart from one end to another? Do we appear as gentle people, or persons who would respond to soft treatment?

The basic purpose of the UFO people, the propaganda of their scenarios, is to indoctrinate their contactees and the contactee audience with concepts and purposes compatible to their own.

In conclusion:

The UFO people are not giving us scientific facts; they are giving us ART, the art of dramatic presentation. It is all done for effect.

They are able to utilize means we do not understand and through the confusion thus created, and the emotional impact, they can change our thinking almost unnoticeably, thus directing us into paths they want us to go.

Contactees, and those who listen, are being shaped, molded, guided, pushed into a future which the UFO Planners have chosen for us.

Should we listen? Should we allow ourselves to be recreated according to their patterns? What right have they to manipulate the people of the Earth?

Do they come at this particular time because we are so vulnerable? We are disenchanted with the social—economic- political world we see around us, the wars, the famines, the treacheries. Religious traditions have set up a dogma of The Coming Judgment, The Last Days, and Armageddon. Scientists speak of earth changes and catastrophes of many kinds we are to undergo. We are ripe for exploitation by anyone who can make us believe that they are "our superiors from outer space" sent to save us from this miserable world we have created for ourselves. In short, to save us from ourselves, for we find we are too feeble to undo what we have done. Our hearts and souls cry out for help.

Silvery ships from the sky, unseen heralds, promises of remedy and salvation—how seductive! We have only to believe in them, to have faith—to allow them to change our thinking on how the world should be run.

Our changed thinking will then change our social institutions, our governments, our religious understanding, for it is from our ways of thinking that these establishments arise and derive their powers, be it in democracy, a communist state, anarchy, or a primitive tribal community.

Are the UFO people creating the world they want to come to before they come?

Why come, annihilate, subjugate in bitter destruction and turmoil, when they can do it all first through art? Perhaps there are too few of them for open combat, but those few of such capabilities and talents that they can accomplish their purposes in this more hidden, velvety manner.

Is it not wise then to consider how they are using those talents to make their way into our thinking, and thus into our institutions and our world, before they openly show or declare themselves?

Perhaps the result, the intent, and purposes of the UFO personalities would be to our benefit in bringing peace on earth, but in permitting ourselves to be so changed and directed we give up our sovereign rights to govern ourselves, to be responsible for our own souls. Nice as the New Order might appear to be, we become, if not slaves, at least second-class citizens.

If it should be true, or have been true, that the UFO persons have interacted with us in previous ages to shape and direct our destiny, has the outcome of that interaction been a thing of peace and glory? Where do we stand now because of that interaction?

They say they will not permit nuclear war. Perhaps they do not want Earth all cluttered up with radiation when they come. They prefer it nice and clean.

If we hand our bruised and bleeding world over to their tender, loving care asking, "Help", can we be sure they will eventually hand it back to us saying, "Here now is your life and world all mended and cozy. Take good care of it." Or will they say, "But you gave it to us of your own free will; you could not care for it." Then we will find the alien on Earth is ourselves. When we give our minds and our thoughts over to alien ways and alien changes, WE BECOME THE ALIEN.

In the beginning we mentioned the element of absurdity or seeming delusion or outright fabrication that sooner or later comes in to the experiences of each contactee, as though his story is being sabotaged and invalidated. Could this be truly an attempt by his captors to thrust him away from overmuch dependence upon them? Are they looking for collaborators, not a welfare state?

Perhaps the great reason for discrediting the contactee is that after so long a period of induction into the mysteries he has come to the point where he may guess or reveal certain secrets that the UFO people do not want revealed. The moment that his understanding becomes a potential threat to that which they prefer — and intend by all means — to keep hidden, in that moment he becomes invalidated and discredited to his own people.

He guesses too much, knows too much, or has come to a place where he may put 2 + 2 + 2 + 2 + 2 together in the near future. "Off with his head", says the Red Queen.

Always I find two, three, or more reasons for each activity of our UFO "friends".

By these intrusions, the total audience effect of the superficial story is weakened, blurred, wiped out, and thus prohibiting the possibility of a build-up of HARD CORE PANIC. Skepticism and doubt remain the final audience reaction but their minds have been set in motion; they wonder and wait.

The effect of character development has been fulfilled. The contactee is now expected to stand on his own two feet, become his own man, and become at last able to function in a more sane and sensible manner in a real and disheveled world.

Our later paragraphs here are meant simply as a caution. Before we crack our foreheads on the sidewalk before the UFO persons, let us ask them, and ourselves, to clarify the role they, the Processors, play in the drama, the GREAT CONTACTEE HOAX in which the contactees, and subsequently the audience, are the VICTIMS.[1]

Notes on "The Great Contactee Hoax"

Symbol and allegory are "put over" or gotten across to the contactee by predominately psychic means, by enforced illusion and hallucinations, hypnotically induced, and by telepathic and sometimes verbal or oral communication, also engineered by hypnotic means. A smaller portion, however, is certainly actual physical event.

---

[1] Proceedings, Rocky Mountain Conference on UFO Investigation (Contactee Conference) May 22-24,1981, Laramie, Wyoming USA

Underneath the surface scenario we look to find the basic theme, or themes, for these are a geometric conglomerate of theme, branching off into many relevant issues and purposes.

An effort must be made to devise a dictionary of reason behind the elements of the scenarios, and thus to decode the pattern of the myth

Why each contactee was told a specific detail was based on what he already was, and this element lays the contactee story open to suspect, as though it is something evolved from the recesses of his own subconscious. Not so, the detail was presented because somehow the UFO Planners are able to discover what lies in the subconscious or past life of the contactee, and to draw from his own resources the elements they need for his own individual "myth".

When we know what each element of the scenario meant to him specifically, we will find that in all scenarios these specifics will repeat, and repeat, and repeat, until the many-avenued pattern of the underlying theme will be apparent. This does not mean the surface facts of his story; it means the decoded elements of his personal myth.

Without the priming he might have had a choice of a half dozen typical reactions. Reinforced by the priming, one reaction became dominant and was carried out as the Planners had anticipated.

One instrument of such priming might have been an object seen on or near the craft, if there were such observances in his initial point of contact.

His choice of action was narrowed and reinforced. It was not distorted nor compelled. By such subtle means the Planners gained their objective, whatever it might be, while the contactee could feel he was acting with entirely free will, completely on his own.

In short, something in the UFO experience reinforced the contactee's future activities, not in an entirely new direction, but in a renewal of a former objective or in the intensification and clarification of a current one. His life's goal and method of attainment was illuminated by the event, not by any directive he was given, but by something he saw. What was his outstanding visual impression? How does it relate to his life's goal?

We are speaking of his initial contact, and for some contactees this is still hidden from conscious knowledge.

This initial contact is Act 1, Scene 1 of our scenario, and it is in it we have found all of the necessary basic ingredients of drama: time, place, setting, the protagonist UFO, the antagonist contactee, his character and background and traits, and the individual story problem.

They use the ideas we already have to put across their message. Therefore, if the events magnify our religious or other beliefs, it does not necessarily mean the UFO personalities agree with these traditions or rules. They simply do not oppose our having them. Each to his own.

In each episode of the scenario they try to make us face ourselves, to make us learn something about ourselves, and at the same time, something about them.

For all of this audience we see the general purpose of each contactee drama, and subsequently of all contactee scenarios, is a processing, a making ready. This is the reason why events are planned as though acts in a drama. This is why a contactee often feels the encounter is hazy and dreamlike, not quite real. It is real enough, but it is not reality, it is an allegory with facets often presented through symbology.

CHAPTER NINE

The Contactee Network

HWEIG AND ASSOCIATES

In the past, contactees have been deliberately kept apart by a number of ploys and ruses.

Each was told to guard the material they had been given, to wait for the "signal" to release it. Each was made suspicious of other known contactees. The topics of material given each were so unique it did not seem to coordinate with any other. Each contactee, when nearly ready to "come out" was made to appear strange, disordered, ridiculous, thus making his own validity suspect. Each contactee was given only a portion of a puzzle; the key to unlocking its full meaning was deliberately withheld. Each contactee was given both sides of a problem, the yea and nay, without being shown how to polarize the two. This kept him confused and off balance, never able to reach any certainty. Contactees were "teased" just enough to keep them skeptical of the purposes of their informant. Some were warned against forming cults or any group which would involve comparisons and exchange of their given material, so that no complete fitting of patterns could take place. Contactees were made to forget the cohesive parts of their material. These were left buried in the subconscious, barring slippages in dreams or hypnosis, until the day of "revelation" would be at hand. Contactees received overt warnings, threats, adjurations to remain silent, to reveal their experience in no public manner, thereby cutting off the possibility of material being shared and compared too soon.

But quietly, underneath all this camouflage, subterfuge, and general concealment, a quiet, steady, sustained, coherent network was forming, partly through the machinations of the UFO informants and their colleagues, and partly through the understanding, analysis, and retention of ideas by the contactees themselves. More and more rapidly, and always steadily, the network was taking form, day by day, minute by 140 minute, ALL OVER THE WORLD, unseen, unknown, unguessed until in the past year there began to surface here and there, always quietly, always subdued, but always steadily, evidence that such a network did exist and was deliberately planned by the UFOlk themselves with the yet unconscious collaboration of the contactee.

Here and there the threads of the network begin to show, the elaborate skeins of significance that tie one contactee to another, and the vital juncture points, the knots of world significance, vital to the future well-being of all of earth's inhabitants, and perhaps of those mysterious inhabitants of unseen worlds as well!

The threads of the network begin to emerge and the knots of the juncture points to show.

On the skeins of space and time, from the far edges of the world, from the cold Artic to the cold Antarctic, from the streets of Bombay to the island of Tahiti, to the hills of San Francisco, so stretches the network of contactees, their experience and information they have been given. From the first day the seed of humankind was planted on earth to the last hour of today, the threads were formed. As gossamer as a spider web, as opaque as a silken thread, as solid as a steel beam, so grew the strength of the threads.

Formed from the cultural environment in which they came to be, each thread was an interpretation of the meaning of life and the universe relative to that contactee's time and place.

As the threads formed and strengthened, the network became active in the lives of the contactees and their audience, however small or extensive that might be, and however hidden the responsibilities of the thread might be. They are there. The network is formed, each thread in place and viable, around the world and back again, each relative to its time and place in the geometric sequences of human endeavor.

In the beginning the threads were relative to Humankind and his relationship to Nature.

The threads now being formed are relative to humankind as World Being, and will stretch into the future of humanity as Cosmic Being.

The network contains the threads of humanity in the aspects of his physical instincts and needs: relief from biological needs, hungers, desires; release from environmental stresses, pressures, disturbances or discomforts; physical contact with other humans; his physical safety and well-being. It contains the threads of emotional/psychological human and his needs of self-identity and will; understanding, sympathies, and acceptance; and his emotional security (from here came gods and authority figures of all kinds). It contains the threads of mental/intellectual human and his needs of self-realization, experience and growth; communication; problem solving work and significant accomplishment (significant in the eyes of the world). It contains the threads of spiritual human and his needs of spiritual identification, recognizing his relationships to spiritual "realities" as they exist for him; collaboration in spiritual understanding, studies, action; and his ideas of endurance through time, immortality, reincarnation, or other beliefs.

The juncture points or "knots" of the network are the places or ideas where various contactees can compare and bring together their individual experience and information. Each contactee will find he has juncture points with many other contactees, but there is a definite distribution pattern, a definite DESIGN to the network. It is not a helter-skelter disarray of tangled threads.

The juncture points are partly socio-cultural, partly environmental, partly historical-traditional, but there is a hidden factor, which is only now beginning to emerge into view. This is the cohesive factor or force that ties it all together.

It is a new understanding of humankind's place in the Cosmic scheme of things, and is being revealed in: the emergence of knowledge of PSYCHIC realities which have been thought of previously as magic, or occult, or superstition; through quantum physics and the emerging new mathematical interpretations, the new revelations of Man's place in the physical universe of "things"; and through a science/religion - religion/science which will become more obvious in the near future, but which is slowly coming into notice even now.

Almost every contactee experience is the manifestation of a myth known somewhere and repeated daily in the world. It is through myths that people see the unseen and understand what is indescribable. Only through symbol and allegory, the language of myths, can the indescribable be known. And that is the secret of the bizarre events of the UFO experience. Yet, behind every myth there is a Reality! The myth, the symbol, the allegory tells the untellable, but the True!

We can take a quick look at some myths too well known to need lengthy exposition:

- The myth: Plato's story of the androgyne.

  The experience: The contactee's experience of dealing with androgynous beings.

- The myth: Apollo and his sun chariot

  The experience: Blazing UFOs and golden haired Venusians

- The myth: Herodotus story of the Phoenix

  The experience: Phoenix seen used as reincarnation symbols

- The myth: Pillar of fire (Bible)

  The experience: Whirling balls of flame or light

- The myth: Talking dolphins or fish (Oriental)

  The experience: Aquatic beings from the sea

- The myth: Hare on the moon, mixing the elixir of immortal life in a stone mortar (Japanese)

  The experience: A trip to the moon, drinking liquid from a stone vessel of a pyramid shape (The UFOlk use pyramids as symbols of initiation.)

Why are contactee experiences often so frightening? Because we are not ready to grasp the significance and purpose of the experience. We are being made ready even as we are given the experience. For each experience there are many meanings and levels; here we follow the network level.

We might sketch the anatomy of a myth so:

A.   Action. What is being done?

B.   What does the action portray?

C.   What is the source of this portrayal? The source exhibits one of the basic needs of physical/psychological/intellectual/spiritual Man.

D.   What is the purpose of this portrayal?

E.   What is the subjective effect, immediate or latent, on the contactee and his audience?

F.   What objective action does he take, or what reaction occurs?

G.   What truth is revealed?

In the myth of reincarnation, the action is that of a Phoenix burning and life arising again from the ashes. The portrayal is of death as the consuming of a body, followed by rebirth in a new body as life goes on. The source of the portrayal was the fear of death, or man's need to resolve his relationship to the hereafter. The purpose of the portrayal was to banish the fear of death. The subjective effect on the contactee was at first fear of the event, then after study, the gaining of confidence and courage. The objective action was to go forward into life with greater assurance that there is meaning and purpose in life even beyond death. The truth revealed was that humankind is not alone nor abandoned, that plans have been made for a survival.

In the myth of the flaming chariots and the handsome blond gods or super-beings the action was communication between them and earth people. Portrayal was of someone who was aware of our problems and was concerned with our future. Source of the portrayal was our fear of being alone in the universe with no super-power to watch over us. This came from the need for gods or authority figures. The purpose of the portrayal was to reassure earthlings that someone cares and can help, someone with great power and knowledge. The subjective effect on the contactee was to build confidence and courage. The objective action taken was to go staunchly forward to "spread the good word". The truth revealed was, once again, that humankind is neither forsaken nor alone.

In the Biblical myth of the flaming pillar that went before the people of Israel, its purpose was to guide. And so in the contactee experience of balls of whirling flame or light. Portrayal was of a guiding light. The source of the portrayal was the fear of losing one's way, the need for superior guidance. The purpose was to reassure that one will be guided and aided. The subjective affect was immediate awe and fear, followed by reassurance that one could be correctly guided. The objective action was to go on with courage and determination. The truth revealed again was that Man is not forsaken, great and knowing powers guide.

And so the examination of each myth and experience comes to one end, the reassurance that we are not alone; SOMEONE cares; help will be forthcoming. This final revelation may be well hidden in troublesome and even frightful events, but the analysis carried to the final conclusion will come to the same understanding each and every time. Humanity is neither abandoned nor alone. And in the final conclusion the myth and the experience become one.

As we said earlier, as the contactee/researcher comes to analyze and understand the contactee experience and to compare one with another contactee, he will begin to see a definite pattern of distribution in types of experience. This is NOT a geographical distribution, but one made patent by the character attributes of the contactees.

This could call for a very complex in-depth analysis of contactees, but we shall not attempt it here, but shall slide slickly over the surface, not wanting to get bogged down in tedium.

It is sufficient to our point here to draw a broad outline of contactee character which will be immediately recognizable to any researcher.

First there is the contactee totally devoted to service. Often this is the proverbial little old lady in tennis shoes, a rather naive doll who obstinately intends to do her bit for humanity, come hell or high water.

Then there is the earnest, dedicated seeker of truth who will spend uncountable hours tracking down each bit of Information.

There is the adventurous "bull it through" fellow, male or female, with an uncanny ability to "roll with the punch".

What we are actually saying here, in a converse sort of way, is that the experience a contactee has is dependent on the kind of character he is.

This would indicate the one who pre-planned the experience for him must have pre-known what type of character he was, and must have equally pre-planned the exact spot in the network in which he would find his place. Thus the contactee is seen not only to have had a significant experience, but one with a definite purpose for his future.

Values of the network to the contactee as a private person could mean a way of fulfilling his basic needs: finding his place in his immediate environment, or changing his environment; becoming absorbed in his own value and meaning; looking for productive relationships with other contactees; readjusting his life direction or intent; strengthening his will and motivation; re-assigning his hours to more productive ends; gaining in self- confidence and courage; re-affirming faith in some greater power or plan or purpose.

How many contactees in the United States alone, even now, are restructuring their lives because of a UFO contact? I am sure we would ALL be surprised to learn that number!

The value of the network to the World Human could mean: gaining understanding and knowledge through comparisons with other's experiences; consolidating work with others, through apportionment of studies, saving time and energy for all; learning many facets and values of experience in addition to one's own; extension of knowledge through parallels, analogies, and repetitious patterns.

The value of the network to Cosmic Human: the contactee views the person s/he is to become, the culmination of the whole process. He sees his personal place in the universe, the Cosmic scheme; his relationships to beings from other planets, other time worlds, other energy worlds, and parallel (spatial) worlds; he sees his significance to infinite/eternal verities and realities, in contrast to their significance to him.

We have viewed the contactee network as a meeting place of contactee experience. The threads are modern manifestations of earth myths, revealing the meaning of life and the universe to physical/psychological/intellectual/spiritual Man. The knots where the contactees' experiences meet and tie together do not mean an over-lapping of a same experience, but a meeting of contingent ones. That is why each is so different. The cohesive factor that ties it all together is a new understanding of Man's place in the cosmic scheme of things through the emergence of new psychic realities, quantum physics and extended mathematics to explain the universe of "things", and a science/ religion - religion/science which will emerge in the near future. The distribution pattern is manifested by the character attributes of the contactees.

As long as researchers look for repetitive patterns of experience, they are going in the opposite direction. They must find their patterns for research in the basic character of the contactees, and mostly in their patterns of belief. But that is another theme for another time. Perhaps this is the time and place to bring the network into the open, and to attempt to find our place in the overall phenomenon.[2]?

To avoid mind control or dissociation:

- Accept the actuality of what is happening,

- Don't try to "divorce" self from the event or a situation that is a series of events,

- Absorb the reality of every moment, live in the NOW, analyze it to self as it happens, articulate to self what is happening as it is,

- Don't do one thing and be thinking about something else. Keep it all together.

But what happens if you don't keep it all together? You dissociate from the event. Let us address this problem of dissociation.

Why do minds "divorce" themselves? How can you control your own dissociation? What is dissociation? What can it lead to? How to direct dissociation into mind exploration under your controlled direction. How to avoid—or invite—mind control.

The door to all psychic phenomena is hypnosis, which results in mind dissociation. You can take this road into either direction. To avoid mind control you must learn how to avoid dissociation. If you have traveled too far on the road of psychic experience and become lost or terrified or out of control, then take the direction of controlling your own mind so it cannot dissociate easily.

If you want to explore the psychic realm and feel you have adequate guidance and protection, then practice mind dissociation.

The more quickly and easily you can dissociate, the more deeply and readily you can enter psychic experience.

To test your susceptibility to mind control, that is, the ease with which you dissociate, experiment with the following:

Place a mirror on the table about a foot in front of you. Let the room be in dim or no light, but put a candle on either side of the mirror. Seat yourself comfortably and relaxed. Stare into the mirror without blinking until your reflected image begins to separate into two images, which begin to draw apart until they reach the outside you have practiced this a few times, clock the time, first from the time you start to stare until the images reach far apart. Secondly, until the images first begin to separate. The lapse of time on each of these indicates how easily you dissociate and how easy or difficult it is for you to be mind-controlled.

If you want to learn to dissociate readily, and thereby open yourself to psychic experience more easily, you can practice letting the image split in two.

If you want to avoid dissociation and thus avoid psychic experience and the concomitant dangers of being mind-controlled, then each time the image starts to split, force it by your mind (not by blinking) back into one image.

That is the beginning experience (not experiment) to let you know where you stand psychically. Which direction you choose is up to you. BE CAREFUL!! If you feel strong enough or when you are ready practice both roads to give you instant control.

Let us try to delineate some of the factors that lead to involuntary dissociation.

First, what is dissociation? It is simply being conscious in two dimensions at once: Your everyday practical necessity-to-survive conscious dimension as well as your psychic dimension, which is the Interdimension between the physical and the spiritual.

Watch out for daydreaming, fantasizing, hallucinogens, esoteric practices; it is easy to get lost if these are carried to extremes.

The avenues of involuntary dissociation are many. One, not altogether involuntary but certainly sub-conscious, is the manner in which we are prone to "divorce" ourselves from unpleasant events and memories. Having been abused as a child, and the practice of trying to separate oneself from the effects or facts of the abuse, is one of the strongest and quickest ways to mind dissociation.

Much has been written on this recently so we won't go into clinical detail except to point out that child abuse takes many forms from actual sexual or physical abuse to emotional abuse of the unwanted or unloved child. Sometimes the child's feeling of abuse comes simply from misunderstandings and lack of communication or the inability of the parents to demonstrate their affection. The effects are the same for the child, a withdrawal from the "reality" of the perceived abuse into a dissociated part of the mind. Such a person becomes very susceptible to all kinds of psychic manifestation and mental disorders.

Another unpleasant event from which we are prone to "divorce" ourselves is the long time wrangling and quarreling between husband and wife in an unhappy marriage or in some other bitter relationship. Rather than divorce the spouse, or other, we divorce a portion of our mind to dissociate our Self from the anguish of the situation. All such basic problems can create the feeling and intent to divorce oneself from the situation and again a process of dissociation is set into motion, the kind and degree inherent in the situation of the individual.

A bittersweet love affair without hope of reconciliation or consummation can be the avenue to dissociative involvements and problems. Job or career aspirations denied and with long time brooding over it are another. A parent's long-standing problem with children, or children's problems with parents, can reach a final point of discouragement.

Death of hope in any direction of life's desires and the subsequent desire to divorce oneself completely from a situation that is, in essence, for one reason or another inescapable, is a summary of the "divorce wish". Because we are unable to divorce the situation, we divorce ourselves and become dissociated, easy prey for any psychic or mental disturbance that introduces itself, or that we concoct for ourselves as an escape route—fantasy, day dreaming, immersion in too deep or the wrong kind of meditation to the exclusion of a sensible balance of more prosaic (life survival) thought.

Other doors are: to be a witness or participant in any incident too traumatic to accept: a grim memory that won't erase, a car or plane accident in which people were horribly mutilated, a rape, a witness of violence to children, accidental or otherwise.

There are initiators to mind control who devise events such as this to purposely bring about a desired effect: the dissociation of another individual, thus opening the door to ongoing psychic events or/and mind control.

The road of dissociation and psychic experiment may be entered upon knowingly and willingly but with many safeguards, pre-preparations and full understanding.

In an initiation the first act of the initiators is to separate the individual from his partners, families, members of the community, because they intend to commit acts of terror upon the luckless initiand, and by finding himself all alone and beset, his trauma can take him to what he believes is the door of death itself. Mentally, emotionally, sometimes with violence, he is brought to the threshold of his endurance. He may all but actually die. To combat the unbearable trauma he will fight to elude the event and the effects of the event upon his mind, to forget, and to escape by dissociating his own mind. Now he has been made ready, opened to the psychic manifestation/teachings that are to follow.

He has lost a substantial part of his mental self-control. If the first act of violent intrusion does not bring about results as strongly as desired, there will be other subsequent violent intrusions until he has been made ready for the instruction to follow.

Our second lesson or experience to avoid mind control is to practice rationalizing the traumatic event, to analyze the contents thereof and assign them the kind and amount of recognition they deserve, no more.

In initiatory terror this calls for analysis of the terrifying event, tearing it into its separate pieces and confronting each piece, not confronting the whole. That is too overpowering; it was so purposely invoked. By confronting each piece one by one, it is possible to gain mastery over the whole.

All of this may be applied also to those traumatic events in our lives that have caused us to dissociate or bring us to a condition where we may dissociate far more easily than is desirable.

Recalling the event, facing it in as much detail as possible, is the most difficult part of the whole process. Breaking it up into bits and processing each bit in turn is the only way to release the fear and terror that was engendered during the event. To gain strength and power in such a practice one must divide and conquer according to a pattern in a useful direction of inquiry. Let us try to establish some basic element of such a pattern.

Don't try to recall the incident as a whole or recall the totality of the emotional or mental trauma. Each time you do so only imprints the trauma more deeply. Divide and conquer.

Divided Pattern of Recall of Traumatic Event

For practice:

First, select an incident you recall from your past that has continued to haunt and harass you, an incident so trivial it should not even be remembered, but for some reason it does, causing you a feeling of embarrassment or shame. Did you actually trip and fall on your face at your first piano recital—or some such thing that should have been minor and long forgotten?

Let us destroy the effects of that incident.

- Concentrate only on the ceiling, roof, sky or the upper reach of whatever covered that event. Articulate, out loud if possible, the description of that overhead covering. The sky was blue and clear. It was cloudy and dark. The ceiling had a pattern of circular design made of plaster. Overhead were lights so bright one couldn't look up. Etc.

- Is there anything overhead to cause you discomfort or pain? No need to remember it. Erase it. Don't just forget it; erase it. Take a blackboard eraser in your mind and wipe it out. It's gone. That part of the incident need never be recalled.

- Look to your left. What is there? A red velvet curtain? Or, outside—two evergreen trees about your own height, dark and thick? A row of folding chairs? Why do you need to remember these, they have no emotional, mental feeling for you. They are useless. Pick them up and toss them down a gully, into the basement, into a garbage container. Throw them away. Mentally perform some definite act that will eliminate them. Forget them, they are useless.

- What is on your right side? Proceed as before

- What is behind you? Proceed

- What is underfoot?

- What is in front of you? A piano? Inspect it. Is it big and dark and gleaming? Is it painted white? It is an upright piano? Is it a baby grand? Look at the keys; are they exceptionally yellowed? Pick it to pieces item by item, the bench included. You can't remember much? Make up something. We are going to rub the whole thing with chalk. Look at the effect. All wiped out and gone. It is useless. Make it vanish.

- What is outward, in the room or landscape? An audience? Who do you see whom you know? Your mother? Father? Aunts, cousins, friends, neighbors? Where are these people now? Do you see them every day? Do you ever hear from any of them? Are they all scattered and gone from your life? Why hang onto this old picture of them? It is useless. Rub your eyes and they will disappear. Wipe away that picture. No part of that picture can touch you in any way now. Wipe it out.

- Wipe away, discard, and throw out bit-by-bit any other part of the scene that recurs to you. Perform a definite obliterating act; don't just deny it.

- Now look at yourself as you were. How are you dressed? Do your shoes hurt? Won't your hair stay combed and in place? Do your shoes squeak when you walk? Are your clothes too tight, too loose? What are the colors? Are they new or are they your Sunday school clothes? Are you comfortable in them? Does your nose itch? Do you feel like coughing? Are your fingers cold? Now look at yourself as you are now and answer the same questions.

How many of the first row of items are still with you as you run over the list the second time? You won't have truly hung onto a single one. Are your fingers still cold? Blow on them, sit on them, warm them. Then know that they are not the same as the fingers from the first scene. Every cell in your body has changed since then, not once but many times. What is there in that old traumatic incident that is still alive today? The old scene is totally useless. The person that was then is also totally different today. Take the eraser and erase the scene. All gone. Where are the sights and sounds and smells and voices? Treat each one remembered in turn. Discard, erase, the scene totally.

Another day "does" another scene, equally innocuous. This does not mean you will never remember them again. They will rise up in a vision before you. But the psychological imprint, the pain and embarrassment, will no longer work to control you.

Go on to more serious incidents, more traumatic, more painful or frightening. Keep using this practice until you are able to undertake demolishments of your most frightful or embarrassing remembrances and to be able to do it quite easily and quickly. This may take a long time, weeks, even years. But the remembrance and effect have been with you for years. It will take time.

You may never entirely forget the pain and fear or hate and disgust but you will have gained mental and psychological power over the effects, even the severe and terrible ones, which have caused you to dissociate.

As you go through the exercises remember to talk out loud to yourself. Articulate every bit of the scene and every movement you make. This is of great importance to imprint the knowledge of what you are meaning to do with the process. When you discard or wipe out some bit, dust off your hands and say with great satisfaction, "There, that's rid of, that's gone." See nothing in your mind but a blank. "That's gone."

Don't do the same scene over and over. Avoid impressing it more deeply. Even if one practice was not altogether satisfactory go on to another. As your power of erasure increases, the early incidents will continue to fade out.

You are not denying or burying the recall of the incidents; that would only cause future problems. You are totally eliminating them from your acceptance. Even if the scene recurs, the power it has upon you will diminish to the vanishing point.

As you gain power of control through these exercises you will build up the power of control over any attempt of your mind (for whatever reason) to dissociate. Hypnosis will become more difficult and mind control from totally human intervention will become impossible.

For the extremely traumatic circumstances that involve crushing emotional power, these require another approach in addition to and after the preceding eradication process. Too many psychological scars and emotional habits are involved. It is difficult to demolish the really heavy stuff without professional help. We can make a start by examining our psychological and emotional self. Our own rational and mental approach can help.

Experiential Practice (Understanding and Pity)

If the current problem of dissociation was caused by an event of violence and irrationality on the part of a person or persons, lay your trauma upon a shelf for the present and seek professional services to HELP YOU UNDERSTAND THE PERPETRATOR. Not to deal with your trauma and not to understand his or her motives but to understand the soul anguish that permitted that person(s) to commit such an act. Then with pity and abstinence from judgment, prayerfully deliver him into the hands of God. You do not have the wisdom or responsibility. Give him to God along with your pity. NOT SYMPATHY for that creates a too close emotional tie, which is most unwise and unsafe. It would only undermine the mind power you need to overcome your own trauma and its resultant dissociation. These will begin to melt away as you wipe your hands and say, "I leave him (her) to God." To dwell upon or try to analyze your own trauma only implants it more deeply. It will dissolve of its own accord in time.

If anything of the original event returns to haunt you just say, "This is no longer my problem. I don't have to deal with it." And deliberately start thinking of something else, something pleasant and soothing. You are not burying the remembrance for future trouble; you are disowning it. It is no longer your problem. You gave it to God.

Mind Power

In order to avoid mind control by others, or by events, one must develop the power of one's own mind. At present this study has been pushed aside and forgotten. Now is the time it would be wise to remember it and we write how this may be accomplished: Mind Power to avoid Mind Control. How to keep from being dissociated by events that embellish trauma and fear; how to avoid being hypnotized by all sorts of surrounding media, advertising, books, newspapers; how to be hypnotized only when one is willing and knowledgeable; how to stave off psychic attacks when one is not ready, not knowledgeable, not understanding, not willing. How to develop the mind power needed to control such events according to one's understanding and the desirability of the event. If one wishes to experiment with psychic phenomena to do so only according to the direction and depth desired; to keep control of one's own mind and the direction of one's own actions and experiences; to be in control — Mind Power.

As we have noted in passing, each of the events that has caused us to dissociate a trifle or a lot and thus opened the door to psychic invasion, has been accompanied by and deeply imprinted because of the emotional impact involved.

So it is not enough to erase the factors of the scene, we must also "purify ourselves" from the emotion. We can do this just as the Native Americans do, through sweat baths—or hot showers— emetics, laxatives—anything to flush the impurities out of the system.

Where the Amerindian does this along with prayer (so I am told) we can best carry out this cleansing with thoughts relative to our own minds. Before entering the cleansing room one may offer a short prayer for guidance and strength and after leaving offer another prayer of thanks. But within the room the thoughts should be strictly on what is going on relative to self.

All the while in the shower or whatever process is chosen, one must articulate aloud what the mind's intent in this exercise is. "I am washing away all the pain, hurt, disgust, anger, despair. The pain is running away with the water, down the drain, out of my knowledge. It is leaving me forever. It is going down my arms, my torso, and my legs". Be as specific as you please, but keep talking yourself out of acceptance of this useless emotion. Convince yourself. Don't pray. It is not God's pain you are trying to get rid of; it's yours. It is not God's mind you are trying to cleanse and make powerful; it's yours.

After you come out of the cleansing room, say your little thanks-giving, and then celebrate. Whatever means a celebration to you; a little personal, private celebration to you. Anything to implant a happy, cheerful, self-pleased emotion in yourself in place of the old bitter one. Be good to yourself. Have a real first rate bang up celebration, something to remember. You have brought the several dimensions of your mind together again, closed the gap of dissociation. You have gained another workable practice of Mind Power

Be so severe with your cleansing that you really don't want to do it. It must be severe enough to drain away the anguish of recall. Once is enough.

You may sometimes remember the eradicated scene vaguely, but you won't cringe, your stomach won't turn over, you won't have bad dreams about it. What has not been perfectly erased will gradually fade away. You no longer have any purpose in hanging on to it.

You may have been a victim of some appalling accident as well as witness to it but it will be an easier trauma to erase than one which involved witnessing a violence against a child, whether that violence was an accident, an "act of nature," an insane act, or, as there has so incredibly been, a planned act. The first necessary step is to erase all self-blame or feeling of guilt that one was not able to prevent the incident or to somehow interfere with the violence of it. The greatest trauma here is self-recrimination.

That can be softened only by taking the accident scene apart bit by bit and answering or articulating aloud a series of self-questions:

What were you doing in that area? Was it home turf, a relative or neighbor's house—in other words, did you belong there in any sense, or were you idly passing by, or had you inadvertently walked or driven to the scene? If it were at a relative's or friend's home you would feel a greater responsibility than if you were in a strange neighborhood or while picking mushrooms you had stumbled upon the scene. That would be a social responsibility but would not be as deeply or personally felt as the former. Was the child a total stranger or someone you knew? Here again, the depth of responsibility/anguish would again vary according to these factors. Finding the depth of responsibility may be an alleviating device emotionally. Tragic as the incident was it is the individual's depth of responsibility and measure of real involvement that we must first specify.

Suppose you were in the woods and stumbled upon the scene where a man was beating his stepdaughter unmercifully. At your shout of rage he dropped the girl and ran into the woods. You were too far away and too late to do more than help the girl. You have no personal responsibility whatever only the social compassionate responsibility we each should feel. You subsequently did everything you could to help the girl and to have the stepfather apprehended and charged.

You must make it absolutely clear to yourself you had no personal responsibility. Do not continue to gore yourself with that unnecessary self-recrimination for not having done more. Try to establish the exact kind and extent of responsibility and you will be relieved from your self-imposed trauma. You will feel it receding away from you. You no longer need to carry it so close in your mind. Let it go. Let the feeling of guilt go with it.

To obliterate a sense of shame at not having been more effective to stop or alleviate the violence, let us suppose:

Suppose you had interjected yourself into the middle of the scene. You jumped right in and tried to change matters. What really could you have done? How effective would it have been? Think of all the different but possible scenarios. Could you have hit him over the head with your walking stick without endangering the girl equally? Could you have aimed a kick at a soft spot and positively know you would have landed? If you were armed would he not have used the girl as a shield? As full of anger and frustration as he was would his strength not have been more than ordinarily human? He could have felled you with one blow and gone on beating the girl with increased rage and added vindictiveness at having been interrupted and attacked.

In all common sense and rationality what could you have effectively done? Nothing more than you did. Believe it. Convince yourself and feel the undercurrent of shame dissolving away.

Then, if necessary, erase the scene bit by bit as you have practiced in our first exercise. Erase the woods, the sky, and the trees, closing in on the participants and erasing them.

You may, by this time, actually feel the gap of dissociation closing. It is a very real and physical gap. Then feel the increasing power of mind as the trauma itself ebbs away.

You will still feel a sense of anger and outrage but it will not be directed toward yourself. It will go outward to the perpetrator of the deed. It will not cause you to divorce yourself from yourself.

If you feel there is a buried memory, something hidden in your subconscious that you can't quite remember yet you are sure it is there because of the effect it has had, don't worry about prying out that traumatic memory. Invent one. Imagine such a scene as we have just witnessed or take a story from a newspaper and inject yourself into it; then follow the routine as given. Be very specific and articulate as you recite each bit.

What you are doing is building up your mind power, so it will be able to reject the process of dissociation.

Try to inject all the emotions into your made-up scene that you know you would have felt had you been an eyewitness. Many times newspaper accounts affect us as surely and as deeply as though we had been there. Or borrow a horror scene from a movie or TV, something that touches you deeply, which really arouses specific and strong emotions. If you can't remember a scene that so traumatized you, make one up and deal with it exactly as though it were authentic. Just don't adopt it so thoroughly that you confuse it with reality! Fantasy is dangerous in itself and can itself lead to dissociation unless the mind constantly reassures itself, "This is fantasy". That is why I say use something actually real or seen. "My part is pure fantasy."

Another situation inspiring mind dissociation is the constant wrangling of husband and wife or of parent and child or other close relationships.

You love that other person devotedly; your relationship would be pure bliss—if only they couldn't talk. Pick, pick, pick, nag, nag, nag, whimper and whine until your mind divorces, not that other person, but itself. It dissociates. The more violent the quarrels and the longer they have gone on, the bigger the gap of dissociation. You can get lost, permanently lost in that gap. And you are wide open to any psychic event that comes along, and even to mind control from outer forces or beings.

You cannot cure this situation by talk. You've tried that, perhaps for years. Words only add fuel to the fire. Words create argument, argument grows violent, hearts harden and turn away. You despair of finding a reasonable cure, you grow bitter or morose and divorce yourself, dissociate your mind from the situation.

Self-hypnosis takes over. You fantasize yourself into a different and happier scenario; eventually it can become almost as real as real.

Let us stop this dissociation before it gets that far. Let us go back to that other person you love with all your heart--if only you could get along. You have tried to talk things out, reason things out, listen and understand. But you don't really understand. Something is being held back, something remains that will not be told. Don't try to understand. Listen but don't talk. Try to FEEL what that other person is FEELING. You don't need to know why. Get as close as you can and FEEL. Is it anger? Is it fear? (Most anger is based on fear, fear of losing.) Is it discouragement, hostility, despondency, loneliness, abandonment?

It requires an effort. It requires sacrifice of your own feelings.

Is she sputtering that AGAIN you didn't remember to bring the dog food and the cat litter, and AGAIN you didn't leave the grocery money? Try to get yourself into the emotional mode of the moment. Be mad at yourself that you forgot all those things again. Move into her anger, become part of it. Of course these are not the real reasons she is upset but it is a starting place. Don't talk until she splutters out the real clue as to what lies behind her anger. She will, this night or tomorrow, if you don't argue. Just look at her sweetly, benignly, and let her talk. Feel her anger as she feels it. Don't grit your teeth and wait for your turn. Her turn IS your turn. Wait! Listen!

How you proceed from the moment that she reveals the real clue is up to the individual circumstances. Don't let go of the stance you have reached. Let her anger be your anger, let her thoughts be your thoughts, let her feelings be your feelings.

Feel what she feels.

The problem will unravel from there. Gradually feel the gap of dissociation close in your own mind. You are no longer divorcing yourself from a situation. You are into the situation and becoming part of it. You are understanding. You will be in complete control again, no moment of unwariness can be overtaken by a psychic event from bad dreams to the hallucinatory brand of UFO sightings or unauthorized hypnosis which opens the way to Mind control by some exploitive outsider.

This is a formula that may be applied to many other conflicts of a similar nature. It may be the wife-husband viewpoint. It may be the parent-child, or the child-parent or friend and friend, any of the close personal relationships which have reached the critical point of self-divorce or dissociation.

Another scenario is when one is not able to provide adequately for material necessities, whether one is alone, or more frequently and impellingly when one has a family or others to support.

Here the self-divorce is particularly insidious for self-disgust is a highly aggravating factor.

The formula here first requires restructuring of the self-esteem. Are you losing the family farm to mortgages and taxes? Are you really to blame? Of course not! There are forces beyond anything you might do about it that are creating such catastrophes as this throughout the world. You are caught in machinations of forces that you don't even see. Find those forces, understand them, face them and face yourself relative to them; the old order of things is passing away, the new order has not yet disclosed itself openly.

Suppose the farm and machinery go? There is no place to borrow additional money in the amount you would need. The farm is totally owned by the banks, the government, the IRS.

Count what you have left: four strapping sons, two beautiful daughters, a patient and enduring wife all in good health. Magnificent! You are already a rich man!

Count your material possessions you will have left, write the list out and evaluate them in dollars and cents all the way down to grandmother's button box. (Do you know some fancy buttons are selling for 15, 20 and 25 dollars?)

You don't have to sell your family treasures, your great grandfather's muzzleloader, your mother's quilts, or the housedog and kittens. But evaluate them along with the hi-fi system and the silver. You are much better off than you think. Include everything.

Already you feel better. You have provided the refinements of living once and you can do it again. You are gathering your strength and renewing your confidence. Let land and equipment go. Don't take voluntary bankruptcy, which is a too heavy load. Have an understanding with remaining creditors that someday, somehow they will be paid.

Polish up your self-esteem and set it back on the shelf. Admire it. You know now, as you never did before, who the real enemies are. You can decide now what to do about the situation. Regroup your warriors and plan strategic moves.

There are many groups, organizations, societies who can help in smaller ways. Use all of them; that is what they are for.

In whatever your new enterprise, plow all profits back into the business for four or five years. Sacrifice luxuries and indulgences, everyone work together for a common goal and you've got it made. Stringent living but effective.

Don't borrow large sums of money. Your credit is your own worst enemy. Be willing to start small and go slowly. That is enough personal advice. You see the direction.

All the while you are going through these personal exercises the self-divorce is losing power, the gap of dissociation is closing, closing until the unity of a completely controlled, self-directed mind process is regained. It is possible to even feel a physical snap somewhere in the forehead when that gap is emphatically closed. Believe it or not!

We could continue to analyze other situations that result in self-divorce—prolonged illness, handicaps, loss of loved one, feeling of being under-privileged or boxed in, but these will suffice for the present. Some of them are being well managed by psychological and clinical help. There is one, however, that we cannot avoid discussing, and that is fear.

Fear is the underlying basis of most of the mentioned situations but these are so over laden and hidden by specifics that the base is obscured.

The greatest fear is the fear of loss—loss of anything—the regard or love of others, self-respect, possessions, relationships. It is difficult to heap all the possible fears in one pile and recite a formula to "cure" them all.

If, when we reduce our situation of divorce of self to analysis, we see that we have been hiding something; we must confront it. We have a secret and have divorced ourselves from it for fear of repercussions if it were discovered, the loss of something we value.

It does not really matter what the secret is that prompted us to divorce ourselves from acknowledgement of it. The effect is the same and the resolution is the same.

Drag that secret out into the light of day and drag out the fear of repercussions if it is known. Is it real? Is the repercussion even probable? Would anyone actually care?

Measure the potentials of your fear. Are they really factual? Are you dramatizing the whole affair just a little too much? Reduce the potential to actuality, to what cannot be discarded. Be real.

Confess the secret to the one whose reaction you fear the most. You can't? Get professional counseling. You can't do that either? Do as the King did, dig a hole, whisper the secret into the hole and cover it up. Won't work? It is much too grave for that?

Then select the person who is most responsible for you maintaining your secret. Notice I said, "Most responsible".

He is the one responsible, not you. Give the responsibility entirely to him. Now he has it, although he won't have the slightest idea he has. You have done him no hurt, no harm, and no disservice. He does not have the secret but he has the responsibility that there is one. That is all his. He created the FEAR that will not allow you to disburden yourself.

Now you no longer need to divorce or dissociate your mind because of the secret and the fear. It is his problem, he created the fear situation although he doesn't have the slightest idea there ever was one. Henceforth treat him kindly, be grateful. Enjoy your freedom from that responsibility. You have made a sacrifice for his sake. You have kept the secret and given him the responsibility that there ever was one. This does not mean blaming someone else for anything, it means analyzing why there ever was a secret. A specious argument? Rationalization? Not at all. It is real. Otherwise you could have revealed the secret and given him the hurt and disillusionment the revelation would have caused.

You still have a feeling of guilt? The offense was serious? Perhaps there is a hard little lump of remorse in your chest? You have allayed your fears, given the responsibility for them back where they belong. Now you are free to go for professional help, psychiatrist, psychologist, minister, or priest -- someone who obeys the rules of confidentiality. And, if so inclined, take it to God in prayer. Mea Culpa. You can handle it.

We have discussed briefly how we may become victims of inadvertent dissociation, the tricks this plays on us, and how we may endeavor to regain control of our unified mind.

Now let us discover some of the ways we may create dissociation willfully, direct it into various avenues of experience, keeping fall control, and remerging when desired.

We will not talk at this point about what we think minds are, or energy fields, or imprints, or neurons, or synapses. You can get all that out of textbooks. We are going to talk about practical experiences in the everyday world. To us, as coherent beings, actuality is in the event and not in dissection of brain processes.

Let us go back to our first exercise when we test how quickly and how easily we dissociate, or how difficult it is for us to do so.

Vary the measuring devices. Put the candles behind the mirror. Put them in front. Use full overhead light or no light at all. Keep your nose six inches from the mirror, ten inches, three feet. Remember to PULL the two images of your face together with your mind, not by blinking or closing your eyes or shaking your head. Willfully and purposely bring the two images back to one. Practice with all variations you can think of. Glasses on or glasses off. Practice the control over and over. The CONTROL is the vital part. The control and the understanding of what we are after.

It may take hours and hours or even days to bring that control to pure perfection, but it must be done before we can continue

Don't skip over it or you are in for hot water, maybe seriously.

It is not enough to know what you are doing. You must be able to do it in a snap. This is the most important sentence in this whole writing. Perfect your own control. You can't slough over it or cheat. You must be in perfect control.

This is the basis of your own mind control, your own mind power which will develop as we continue. Do not go on with this until you are able to snap those images together instantly on command. Now YOU are in control.

At this point we are practicing mind control, not ways to slip down avenues of psychic adventure. Control comes first, so let us consider some of the ways we dissociate every day. By calling attention to the fact that we are thinking in two directions at once we can practice snapping back instantly into one direction only, another exercise in strengthening mind power.

Suppose that we are working on some rather boring job or hobby that really does not need all that constant attention. We slip off into daydreaming, musing, or fantasy.

Besides the danger of inattentiveness and possibility of accident, we are permitting our mind to go dallying off without our supervision.

Don't say our subconscious takes over on the job while the conscious mind does the musing. It is all one mind, and at this moment it is dissociating in a mild and presumably innocuous manner. Don't believe that! It is practicing bad habits behind your back. Get it back under full control, one direction at a time.

Someday you will learn after much struggle to think on two, three or four levels all at the same time. But you will know what you are doing, how to control it, and most seriously of all where you are going with it. For now you are disciplining your mind to do exactly what you tell it to and nothing more nor less.

Stop the mind wandering. Come to a stopping point in your work. Go sit down with a cup of coffee and muse to your heart's content. One avenue of thought at a time. For discipline's sake.

Suppose you have been under some severe stress for a long time. Now you are driving down a lonely road at night. Your driving doesn't take too much attention, the road is straight, there is no other traffic; you are just humming along. You are relaxed. Your mind begins to wander from the task of driving; it does not really require much attention. The white line down the center of the road is a little hypnotic. Relaxed after some stress, your mind divided between driving and musing, you are in perfect condition for a psychic experience. Catch this before something weird happens that could upset your life for a long time. Concentrate on the driving only, even if you have to talk out loud to yourself, describe where you are, what you are seeing, hearing, feeling, and doing. Get your mind in full control and keep it there, concentrate on the one line of thought only.

Learn to recognize that such little events of dissociation are ready to come before they actually happen. Control the experience. You are not only controlling the dissociation you are building mind power. You are developing control power. Every day in every way practice controlling a one-track mind. Only with constant discipline can you come into full control. It will take time. It will often be boring.

The day will come when you can do all kinds of fancy maneuvers with your mind but control comes first. Discipline is the key.

At all times be fully aware of where you are and what you are doing and let nothing distract your mind from that. On the bus going home you can do your musing while someone else is driving. If you don't forget where to get off.

Helping Someone Return From the "Psychic Outback"

Psychic invasion reaches the mental through the emotional. First the emotional stress must be lessened and eliminated, and only then can the mental background be dealt with. Relieve the stress through very light hypnosis to keep the mind focused. At first dwell on the emotion only, not the cause. When calmness and peace of mind has been restored then the mental background can be approached. The emotional stress must be seen as useless. There must be a restructure of emotional values. If the emotion is hate, attack the hate itself, not the reason for the hate.

Learn the uselessness of hate. If you try to attack the reason for the hate—or anger or fear first—you only imprint and magnify and make more violent the emotion. Let the victim himself uncover the uselessness of the emotion. When he can say, "I'm being foolish. I'm being silly. This emotion doesn't get me anywhere," then he is ready to discuss the reason for the mental aspects of his situation, and not before. He may not be able to give up his emotion wholly, but he has come to see the uselessness of it, that it doesn't solve anything.

Do not ask such questions as "Why are you afraid (angry, etc.)?" but "How long have you been afraid?" "How often does this fear reoccur?" "What do you do when—?" At all times keep the emotion as the central subject. Attack it from all angles but let the victim do the work. "Does your fear interfere with sleeping? Eating? Social life?" Make him dwell on the emotion and how it affects his life. "Has your emotion ever made you do something you regret?" Pound the emotion to death with questions, until he begins to see the emotion is a detriment, worse than useless, and he would be much better without it.

Once he has confessed to the futility of his emotion, we can ask about the (mental) reason for it.

"You say you fear men because your father beat you when a child? Why did he beat you?"

The project here is to UNDERSTAND THE FATHER. Why was he the way he was? Do not judge or allow for a judgmental analysis. Strive for a compassionate analysis. Dwell upon the father, not the beatings. Encourage the victim to remember better things about the father, to recall anecdotes that reveal other facets of his father's character, even amusing things, let the laughter, then the underlying love or admiration or any positive emotion build up— gratitude, appreciation, respect. Encourage and amplify the positive. Use deeper hypnosis here to help recall all the positive and good things which have been buried under the fear until the magnitude of the fear has decreased and been balanced out by good remembrances. This may take a long struggle but the fear has been there a long time.

Now that the fear has been seen to be useless and remembrance of the father has been balanced by positive factors, the attention can be turned to the generalized fear of men that has hampered and distorted this person's life.

A person in a "mental" hospital is one who has been said to have "lost his mind". He has acted in an irrational or mindless manner, that is, through an emotion or reaction rather than normal rational, mental comprehension of acceptable human values. He is emotionally and mentally displaced. Sometimes this state has been reached because of chemical imbalance in the system and the condition can be alleviated by medical treatment. Sometimes it is the result of traumatic events in the person's life which has sent him "over the edge" of reason.

To try to reach the mental aspects, the thoughts, ideas and beliefs first is unnecessarily aggressive. Only after the emotional trauma is alleviated can the mental be approached in a calm, re-laxed, and non-intrusive manner.

A person who has reached the point of institutional re-straint has a much stronger and resistant trauma to overcome than the psychologically disturbed person just described. But the direction of help must also be first toward the emotional cage in which he has entrapped himself.

He has no emotion or shows no emotion. Don't believe it. He has deliberately dissociated himself, divorced himself from the feeling any emotion.

Here you do not directly attack his emotional state, or his mental state. You attack the dissociative state. He has taken himself into a "psychic outback" from which he must be returned. He may be having numerous psychic disturbances, hearing voic-es, seeing visions, etc. These cannot be brushed aside as non-sense. They are real at least in that they impinge on his reality and cause him to react. In that aspect they are real enough to demand serious attention. They cannot be attacked directly. The fact is, they are experienced because of his dissociation and that can be "attacked" and cured. He has become embroiled in the dy-namics of the supra-conscious without knowing what it is or how to handle it.

I could stop here and write a book on the supra-conscious, but this is not yet the time. I will only mention enough to get this show on the road.

Our man who shows no emotion is not without emotion. He is frozen in absolute terror of what is happening to him. He doesn't dare think about it or allow any recognition to enter his mind or he would dissolve into a screaming banshee. The non-emotional seeming facade is his only defense.

The super-conscious is neither benign nor cruel. It is what it is, a human experience. We must learn what it is and how to handle ourselves in relation to it. But that is another story.

The initial project here is to give our man a point of security. This could be a person or an idea, religious or otherwise. But he is such an intense person the security attachment could be over zealous and thus imply a danger. But not until he feels "safe" can he melt the bars of the cage he has self-created.

Here hypnosis may be used to help him learn to surround himself with a circle of light. No evil can break the circle. Let him come to that conclusion himself and to know that each time he feels threatened he can engender that circle of security. Once he feels there is a refuge for him in time of overwhelming trouble he can gradually be helped to un-braid his tangle of three-level consciousness: his subconscious, the res-idue of his past which has specified his desires and his reactions; the conscious world of everyday affairs, with which he has struggled to cope; and the super-conscious world of forces and design, which he cannot understand and which have allowed him to become terrorized beyond acceptance.

We suggested in the beginning of this—under more mild circum-stances—how to bring the dissociated state under single mind control. Here it will be a longer, more detailed, more gradual process with many detours and slippages, but it can be done.

We offer these above suggestions from our own experiences.[1]

---

[1] Dated 11-19-89

Why Are They Here!

IDA M. KANNENBERG AND

HWEIG, AMORTO AND THE HIDDEN ONE

For the past ten years or longer Dr. R. Leo Sprinkle has been talking about and writing about us becoming Cosmic Citizens.

According to this dictation he is exactly right. Before the UFO people want us cluttering up space and their communities with our destructive and polluting ways, they are trying to teach us, through many other persons and experiences, how to become good cosmic Citizens.[1]

Recently I was asked to speak at the local UFO organization's meeting. My long time communicator, mentor and comrade, asked to dictate something for me to read to the group.

Hweig, Amorto and the Hidden One

We are here, your three helpers, The Hidden One, Amorto, and I. You shall know more about us presently.

We concur that research into the government cover-up would be beneficial, but we three have joined together at this time to guide and steer you on another project.

You have discussed with us that Lindberg's flight across the Atlantic alerted us to the Earth people's development of flight, and that

---

[1] Dated 1989

before a generation had passed flight into outer space would follow. We knew that the conquering of space would mean carry-
ing Earth's contaminations to other planets and peoples. This is
the basic reason for our interference! We do not come so much
to save Earthians from themselves, but to save others from your
pollution. Now do you begin to understand? Put it all together
from that perspective! We are leveling with you. Now tell the
world with your talks and writings.

Save God's children from the pollution and contamination
of Earth!

Does that not solve the riddle of the severe and not so
pleasant things we have done? Does it not explain why each of
those whom we have contacted has seen us in different ways, analyzed us in differing lights, good and evil, angels or demons,
helpful or destructive ones? Each receives us according to his
own inner being, his on light, his own qualities and attributes.

We will not mention names, but there are those who call
us hideous, disgusting, evil, and there are those who call us benevolent, friendly, helpful and good.

As your own soul envisions us, so we come to you, damned
or blessed.

Do you not see that this is why we have played hide and
seek with you, and remain hidden except for momentary glimps-
es just enough to let you know we are here, but not enough to
reveal who and what we really are, or from where we actually
come?

Those of the earth who are in their own soul benevolent
and kind, helpful, generous, and compassionate have been more
clearly told truths about us. Those who are arrogant and self-
centered have been tormented with many tricks and trials. We
try to play back into your face what you yourself are, and from
there to lead you out into what you might become, not for your
OWN sake, but for the sake of the rest of God's creatures, which
too many of you seem willing to destroy and contaminate and
degrade as quickly as possible.

Yes, we are moralistic. Is that bad? What we seek to change are yourselves so as to render your contamination impotent to impinge on the lives of others, those far, far away, or those close at hand.

The world is changing, and rapidly, not the change of political revolution or physical catastrophes, although those things are happening, but more vital, the change in man's thinking. That is the crux and the nexus, the core and the circumference, to change man's thinking from the current dissolution of all that is good and true and beautiful.

Art, music, dancing, painting have turned from the creation of soul enhancing beauty into hideous representations of the basest and worst in man, reverting to the level of all that is most gross and lewd in his being. And the most sublime of the arts, Love, has been debased to jungle lust.

Do you think we, the guardians of the universe, will allow this canker called Earth Civilization to spread into the sweet sanctuaries of the universe?

How many eons have we toiled to bring Humanity from his dirt encrusted beginnings to the finest sensitivities of his soul, witness Da Vinci, Michelangelo, Plato, Gandhi, Jesus, that we should now watch him wallow in the basest forms of self-expression. It is time for the pendulum to swing back toward self-respect and self-discipline. That is what we are here to help regain. Get yourself together, be kind, and be decent.

We have watched the development of flight on earth and have become concerned with Man's development of himself and his civilization. We knew he would eventually extend his capabilities into a flight to the stars. Already he has littered space with thousands of pieces of cast off debris, endangering the lives of others.

Will his conscience allow him to litter the pure, untouched planets with more garbage? Will his contact with other civilizations beyond his solar system bring them the diseases of body and soul with which he is afflicted?

God forbid.

We, the Guardians, watch. We do what we can, what the sacred laws of the universe permit, to change the direction of Man's thinking, so that wholesome commerce and communication may someday, not too long away, traverse freely between your home planet and others which are to become known.

End of Hweig, Amorto and the Hidden One's dictation.

CHAPTER ELEVEN

The UFO Effect

IDA M. KANNENBERG

Do the UFO people not want us to believe what we are being told? What they seem to want is the effect on us because of the telling.

Why confuse the contactees? Why all the camouflage? Why make all the investigators distrust contactees and contactees distrust each other? Is it only because the UFOers do not want 2 and 2 put together yet, they are not ready to blow their cover?

Various kinds of censorship only add to the lack of any coherent put-together.

Out of all this negativism can we derive something positive?

How, in what factors, do all the contactee stories coincide? What are the repeatedly told and affirmed elements retrievable from all kinds of contacts?

No matter how many personages are inventing these stories, or how great their imaginations, if they all come from the same source sooner or later the stories are going to overlap and the same factors repeated 50 times might have some element of truth in them.

I was told, "We cannot fantasize something which has never occurred, or been, or which does not exist as an idea in someone's mind and is about to occur or be".

Every fantasy has an element of reality.

So is it too naive to believe all these made up tales, as told to the contactees, must somewhere, somehow, in some part contain a grain or two of truth?

At what points do they coincide?

What factors are most often repeated?

But this is only a superficial testing. We cannot only go deeper, but we can also devise a method for statistical analysis, not of the contactees, not of the information or messages received, but of the manner in which the episode was constructed, the underlying blueprint.

In the study or analysis of the blueprint for each contactee's experience the reason for each aspect of the experience will become evident. And in the summation of these—in the repetitious themes—will be exposed the purpose of the total experience, and that is the specific purpose of the UFO people.

For the purpose of this analysis the individual contactee is not all that important.

The manner in which he was put through his paces is. This gives us a living organism to work on, not dissected parts of an inert body. (How can you discover life if the corpse is dead?)

The UFO people are presenting material to us that we must dissect on many levels of meaning..

We need not believe 100%, or 80%, or even 60% in what they say precisely as they say it. It is all done for effect believing that is the only way to break through to us with their complete meaning, the only impact they can make, the emotional one.

The dramatic episodes encountered are just that, good drama, purposeful and meaningful on many congruent levels, and must be analyzed as we would analyze drama, structurally.

Many of the incidents of UFO contact have been prematurely revealed through psychological accidents. Had the exposure waited for the timed event, the experience would not have been so unnerving and mystifying to the contactee. All are timed to come to recognition AFTER other preparations and revelations have taken place.

The mental contactees with telepathic experiences do not yet recognize the full dramatic importance of various portions of their experience. That too, is timed to be known later.

Those experiences which were not intended to be known so soon and those still not known were given thus early with the purpose that they would be held in the subconscious of the contactee where the effects would serve meanwhile as directives to conscious action, as guides, and as emotional supports or aids.

The whole UFO production is a dramatization of reality, pictorially presented, subconsciously preserved.

These events were planned to be buried in the subconscious of the contactees for later resurrection. Therefore they were given in pictorial representations for the most part, for the spontaneous or natural recall by the subconscious is mainly pictorial. (The manner of communication among the various UFO people, and they are varied, is by pictorial telepathy). The natural hallucinatory reaction of the subconscious is in definite pictorial symbols. It is from these natural pictorial inclinations of the sub-conscious that the UFO drama is extended.

The major portion of the extended symbology can be found in the deeper studies of the Rosicrucians, or in some part in the secondary level of writing of the ancient Egyptian symbols, for the Egyptian monument writing has several levels of meaning, or again in the deeper levels of Tibetan lore.

Some of the things the UFOs have been telling us are untranslatable into our terms; we have no terms to encompass them. Verbal representation would only arouse intense opposition because of cultural and traditional beliefs. Therefore they resort to drama, symbolism, and metaphor.

In the contactee stories, and particularly in those of the mental telepathy contactees, the messages are but part of that experience. The entire experience, the physical, mental, emotional, psychological, spiritual layers of the experience will help discover the same layers of purpose in the contacts of the UFOs.

Out of all these stories, much conflicting, certain consistencies will stand forth, not the superficial fantasy of "facts" but the elemental thrust of the experience itself. Somewhere there is a key to their purpose, and it will be found in the architecture of the stories rather than in the separate building blocks.

A methodology for scientific examination can be constructed and maintained on this basis. Concentrate not so completely on the contactees, not on the messages obtained; concentrate on the mechanics of the entire episode.

Take one good scholar of Shakespearean drama, a complete manual of Rosicrucian symbology, the complete story of any one contact and the resultant architectural analysis would give the basis of a methodology for studying all UFO presentations.

(Note: It has even been said Shakespeare was a Rosicrucian).

Adamski and his experiences seemingly inside a flying saucer was living allegory, not reality. He reported what he saw and what he saw was a representation of reality, not reality itself. Unfortunately his interpretations thereof became confused with interpolations, misunderstandings and some non-intended adlibbing.

In the Betty Andreasson story the symbols were so uncustomary that the fact they were symbols became readily apparent, and we quickly realize she was going through an illusionary episode, exposing an even deeper reality through symbolism.

The "lies" of the UFO presentations are the "lies" of good dramatic production. Perhaps they truly expected them to be recognized sooner or later as an extension of "poetic license."

In all good drama character change or character development is one of the major vehicles of the story. So in UFO contacts, character change or development has proven to be one of the major aftermath effects of the encounter. This is by no means the end of the drama, when the UFO flies away, or the telepathic voices say goodbye. By the contact the initiate has been inducted into the mysteries of the UFO reality. Influences have been set up that will continue for years thereafter. The climax and denouement and working out of the plot structure are yet to come. But the initial episode has set the theme, the plot line, the emotional tone, the setting, the background facts and all of these basic architectural ingredients ARE THE SAME no matter how expressed, dramatized, symbolized, or stated.

The SUBJECT of each is:

THE UFO EXPERIENCE

The THEME of each is:

We come as friends to give you valuable knowledge that will enrich your life and be of benefit to others.

The EMPHASIS of each is:

A CHARACTER Study

The PLOT STRUCTURE establishes and carries out the reality of UFOs and inter-action with occupants and resultant changes in contactees' viewpoints and life direction.

With CLIMAX AND DENOUEMENT yet to come.

From this skimming of the structural outline we ascertain one of the major purposes of the UFO contact is to CHANGE or DIRECT the LIFE or CHARACTER of the contactee. And that is indeed just what happens.

All of this must be gone into at much greater depth with a more profound analysis and understanding than I am capable of.

An obvious question arises: Why is each contactee, whether by craft appearance or mental telepathy, given such a different story about the origin, reason, meaning, and purpose of it all? Why such a wide divergence of information?

We have already studied a preliminary reason, that each contactee is given a story structured to his own mode of understanding and acceptance. But even with this purpose in mind the stories could contain more overlapping material, and need not be so widely divergent that there is no chance of reconciliation between them.

To serve as a camouflage is probably one of the initiatory purposes of the divergent stories, no one can put two and two together and come up with answers the UFO people are not yet ready to divulge. But there is a possible even deeper purpose than these, a purpose that lies right next to the heart of one of their major purposes in coming.

The stories they tell are partly truth and partly nonsense. The true part is for ourselves to keep. The ridiculous part is to keep us from becoming some kind of a collective unit. Who is going to join forces with someone telling such insane stories, which could possibly be out and out lies? The major effect of their representations is to make each of us stand apart to develop a strong individualism.

They are saying, "We are here. We want you to know it, but we do not want others to believe you when you tell it, so we give you silly stories to relate about our interaction with you, and about ourselves. No one will believe you, but you are now prepared, inducted into our mysteries, you and every one of our contactees."

As a blind collective unit, assembled contactees would be a body of force without a head, dangerous to itself and whatever came close to it.

So the reactionary effect is to try to make the more studious contactees collaborate with others of the same ilk to make sense out of it all. Not a collective unit, but a collaborative force. Each is too wary of the others idiosyncrasies and "fantasies" to adopt a collective stance. But collaborative effort of staunchly individual personalities is the final aim.

So now we have an army of collaborators each trying to make good his own ideas within the framework of the whole. And that does call for great wariness. A man is not as jealous of his wife as he is his ideas. And such a situation can immobilize the whole army by internal jealousies and bickering, until the whole collaborative effort becomes impotent. Those who might have been excellent individual researchers become paralyzed working in the group framework. Yet it is the most productive way, the quickest way, and probably the only way to get anywhere. Therefore the framework is the vital factor to be most energetically considered, and to be outlined from the beginning and held fast to the end. And perhaps that is where no true framework is better than any framework at all. No clubs, no organizations, no cults, no religions, no nothing but a synchronized effort in one direction. Collaboration without rules of order. A framework so tenuous it becomes flexible to any situation, any event, any personality, any catastrophe.

Is this the type of thing they are trying to teach us to do, by their actions and exposure of events, not by advice?

Stand on your own feet, hang onto your own ideas, use them collaboratively with others to make something viable and useful to all, is this the message within all the confusion and camou-flage?

But for what purpose? For whose purpose?

Maybe the fact of collaboration is itself the purpose, and in the final analysis, it is our own.

So we see that each of the conflicting stories of the contactees is valid on four different levels:

A. Camouflage to avoid 2 and 2 being put together too soon

B. The easiest story for each particular contactee to accept and as-similate

C. To keep each one separated, an individual

D. To mold him to the future

While many contactees have not yet knowledge of their contact either in part or in full (probably none in full) the material and its ef-fects lie deep in the subconscious of each where it does inter-relate and inter-act with the conscious self.

Some of the writer/researchers sneer at the caliber of the con-tactees, but who else is so willing to listen and try to be of help, even if it involves personal stress and torment, than little old ladies in tennis shoes, idealistic farmer boys and fishermen? In the beginning the UFOs tried all the approaches to the official, the scientific, the intelli-gentsia and found futility. Direct physical approach met with fear and aggression.

Perhaps their manifold appearances are saying in effect, "We can come to you as monsters and ogres if that is what you want us to be."

"Or we can come to you as benevolent Brethren if that is what you want of us."

"We can appear as whatever you want."

Is this intended as a humble plea for acceptance ON OUR OWN TERMS?

Are these extremes of appearances only symbols hypnotically projected?

When no one listens to the experiences of the mental contactees, when they are tossed in the wastebasket or sloughed off as something not quite nice to talk about, then who keeps any track? Who knows how many there are? Who knows what they, or rather the UFO boys behind them, are up to? They quietly ripen in secret, those who have tried to be heard, and the many more who have never tried for fear of ridicule and harassment.

Who knows how many mental contactees there are, how virile they are individually, how potent they would be collectively?

There is a timing built into the story of each when the real purpose of the contact is to be revealed. The timing is not one of hours, or minutes, or mechanical time, but the timing of need. Whose need? Probably those who put the timing there, the UFO people.

Is the climax of the drama that when the saucers come the contactees will come forward with one purpose, to assist with the landing, a welcoming committee?

Or is the hour of climax timed before the arrival of the ships, when all contactees toss their bits and pieces and clues into the melting pot, and the cumulative evidence results in an acknowledgment and understanding of the full purposes of the UFOs?

With only one possible denouement - the UFOs arriving in peace and harmony?

And is the moral of the story that men must learn to collaborate and work together for the good of all, themselves and their skyward neighbors?

And again, this may not be the climax, the denouement, the moral of the story at all. The climax may be something totally unexpected and unguessed, the denouement extremely undesirable, and the moral - catastrophe!

They do seem to be steering us right in one direction – collaborations!

Appendices

Author Profiles

Amorto: Time Traveler from Atlantis who telepathically dictated manuscripts to Ida. He is a physical human.

Hweig: A Son of Old Atlantis, Hweig was born in 1845 to a time traveler father and Russian mother. Hweig's mother died when he was seven and his father was lost in in time travel, leaving him orphaned. His grandparents living on the Atlantean space island picked up Hweig and reared him until his father returned. Hweig mentored and dictated manuscripts to Ida telepathically. He was a *Sage* similar to those that Ea trained to establish civilization. After an education on Sirius, he returned to the Earth to work in 1940.

Ida Kannenberg: UFO contactee who encountered the time travelers in 1940 and began active collaboration with them in 1977.

Jamie: Time Traveler from Atlantis who telepathically dictated manuscripts to Ida. He is a physical human.

Krsanna Duran: UFO contactee who participated in simultaneous communication with the time travelers and Ida Kannenberg. She developed TimeStar Earth with a geometric model the time travelers mentored in synthesis with elements of Native America's calendar that originated in Atlantis.

Maez: Member of the Arcturian council that monitors Bigfoot on the Earth. Maez mentored Ida when writing her book about *Bigfoot, My Brother Is a Hairy Man,* but did not dictate the book to her. He is a seven-foot tall Gray, with human DNA root.

Rama: A title the time travelers gave to Ida Kannenberg.

The Hidden One: An adept and spiritual teacher who incarnates in a physical body only when he has a specific purpose for a physical life. After knowing him as "The Hidden One" for decades, Ida learned circa 2000 that he is, in fact, Thoth, who was the architect of the Great Pyramid. The acronym of "The Hidden One" comprises the first three letters of Thoth's name.

Tres: An adept and spiritual teacher, who rarely spoke but conveyed a bearing of kindly authority with few words.

Guardians, Creative Forces, the Source,

and the Radiance

About Thoth

You asked about Thoth and Tres. I can give you a brief bit about each of them now and the rest will be in books in progress. Here is a paragraph from *Reconciliation*[1].

My former correspondence with these out-of-this-world characters had settled down to three personages in these later years. There was the perennial Hweig, The Hidden One who now wants to be known as Thoth, and a third. Since number three would give me no name, I have called him Tres. He seldom said more than a few words at a time but he was quite authoritative when he did. He always went straight to the core of a subject without extraneous chatter. From the tenor of his remarks, I decided he must be a highly placed entity. I was encouraged to let my curiosity rest at that, without suspicion. Since Hweig is gone and Thoth has come to the fore in his own identity, Tres has taken a more active role in our conversations.

This is about Thoth and from "Are We Property" which I have barely started.

Thoth: "Yes, Ida, there were humans on Earth at the time of the dinosaurs, 60 million years or more ago. No, not the same strain of human that Maez told you about in your Bigfoot book; your kind of human. These others were the original, straight from God essence, no interference of ET meddling or muddling about with genetic altering.

"They were not made from the red dust of the Earth. That is a metaphor to indicate they were made of the most elemental substance you recognize, from the "material" or pre-substance of the Supra-consciousness, God's direct thought.

---

[1] *Reconciliation-A Study Restoring Man's Faith In Himself And His Place In The Scheme Of Things*, With Thoth, Tres and Hweig. 2004

"Since I, Thoth, the first son or the first human specimen was made of that substance, I can tell you about it from experience.

"At first it was not material as we recognize matter. My body and the bodies of those who followed were made of Light. We had transparent bodies with a "now you see me, now you don't" appearance depending on how we stood in a shadow. As we became accustomed to handling the material of the Earth and interacted more and more with the creatures of the Earth, we too took on a greater substantiality, patterning ourselves after the animals that inhabited the Earth before us.

"We did not mate with animals. God patterned our bodies on their construction as we begged to be allowed to eat food and to drink, and eventually to reproduce ourselves. We brought material being onto ourselves, and once we had tasted the delights of physicality we only begged for more until eventually we were spiritual beings or "souls" encased in physicality. We were the first truly human race on Earth and I whom you know now as Thoth was Earth's first human being, the first "son of God".

"Today I want you to lay aside that understanding and think of me as Thoth the bringer of knowledge of science and medicine and art to my companions by the grace of God."

Dear Karin and Paul,[2]

You asked about Guardians, Creative Forces, The Source, and The Radiance. The reason Hweig did not talk about these is because they are in the spiritual realms and Hweig was assigned to psychic subjects only. The ETS have very compartmentalized jobs. They must stay inside their boundaries and not stray outside.

So I will call upon Thoth to give us some information, as he is a spiritual entity.

THOTH: Yes, this is my department and I'm happy to give you some very brief explanations.

Guardians are those who, like me, watch over persons or projects. We are not physical beings although we can take on physicality for brief periods when it is useful to do so, or we can be walk-ins. Mostly

---

[2] Letters to Karin Hoppe Holloway and her husband Paul.

we try to keep our assigned humans out of trouble and help them to find better paths of accomplishment. Every human being has such guardians. You can call them guardian angels but that brings up images of creatures in long white robes with fluttery wings. We don't flutter. We don't have physical form so we don't feel cold or need robes.

Creative forces use both energy forces and physical forces. They are the active manipulative forces and are energy beings like ourselves. They are what the word Elohim in the Bible was meant to describe. They try to bring about desired events or objects.

The Source is the Creator God who does the programming and gives the material and directives needed for creating. The material is the supra-consciousness of God or the RADIANT INTELLIGENT ENERGY, the first substance from which all else is made.

The Radiance is the active mind of God from which all creation flows.

Love,

Ida

Psychic Research Correspondence with

Dr. Leo R. Sprinkle

May 10, 1979

Dear Ms. Kannenberg:

Thank you for your good letter of April 26th, and for the "outline for interviews in psychic research." I am very pleased to receive the summary, and I hope that you are willing to give me permission to quote from the statement you have provided me. If you do give me permission, I am willing to indicate that the information comes from "Rama", if you do not wish for me to use your name.

I am very interested in your writings, not only because of the possibility that they are received by you through mental communication from UFO personalities, but also because the information given you is very similar to the observations which other people have made who claim contact with UFO entities. Thus, it is almost as if there is some kind of overlap or confirmation of the reliability of the experience. (I am referring to "reliability" as an indication that other people have similar claims; I do not know how to deal with the question of "validity" — that is, whether the information actually does come from UFO personalities.")

I am sending you, under separate cover, the materials in the "Survey of psychic impressions of UFO phenomena." When you have completed and returned the materials, I shall be glad to have them scored and to share with you information about your profile results and how they compare with those of other persons who have participated in the survey.

I appreciate your willingness to share information with me, and I look forward to further correspondence.

Best wishes to you.

Sincerely,
R. Leo Sprinkle, Ph.D.,
Director Division of Counseling and Testing
Professor of Counseling Services

April 26, 1979

Dear Dr. Sprinkle:

Thank you for your letter of April 23rd, acknowledging mine of April 11, and seriously considering a summary review of my experiences. I have told no one about them except my husband, not even my mother who lives with us. All she knows is I spend endless time in my room bending over a hot typewriter.

How does one summarize some 125,000 words! But these are mostly my personal experiences, learning to work with these avowed UFO personalities and passing a few hundred of their interminable "tests, tests, tests."

Perhaps we can strike the heart of your professional interest best by simply sending you an outline of one of their projected books, and of course the most suitable would be the "Outline for Interview in Psychic Research"!

At first they seemed to want me to learn to do psychic research from their viewpoint, but soon realized my forte was writing rather than interviewing, so decided to extend the outline into a book for anyone interested to use.

After receiving your letter yesterday, they added material relevant to UFO experiences specifically.

I am awaiting the copies of your two articles most eagerly, hoped they would come today, but they did not.

Also I am anticipating receiving your surveys and will be quite happy to participate therein.

I am not, by any means, 100% sure of the validity of this experience nor of the affirmations of my communicators. I range from 80% a believer on my up days to 60% on an average, but sometimes on horrible days my belief plummets to zero.

Thank you for all courtesies and consideration,
Ida M. Kannenberg

Psychic Research

HWEIG AND JAMIE

At first we intended this outline to be used in conducting some research and tabulating the information. Now we realize it would take too much of Rama's time to learn to do this and to carry it out with any proficiency. Therefore we are going to deliver it, even more completely than we had intended, and to be a book for anyone interested in such studies to use.

We realize much has been done in your world along these lines, but we believe we have much knowledge and have learned some subtle methods of obtaining information that might be of use to your world. Therefore we shall do the best we can to impart such of that knowledge as we deem would be useful.

Psychic Research, to us at least, is one of the most exciting and rewarding of all studies. We have become Masters in the use of psychic abilities and have vast volumes of lore on psychic phenomena.

For use in your world we have necessarily constrained ourselves to write only of those subject of immediate value to you. Perhaps later, in a few years, we can go into more hidden and esoteric phenomena which you will by that time need to know. We do not say this to tease, only to point out that not all can be done in one single volume and that the subject is extensive and valuable and that we are by no means done with it when we finish this comparatively small volume.

We can go forward most easily and quickly by establishing right here and now that psychic research as it is done in the world today is most superficial and its causes are completely unknown, not even guessed, and the analysis of information gained is therefore not as useful as it might be. A cautious statement indeed, but we are trying not to get carried away in superlatives.

Once we have begun this project we will be able to add some pertinent events which we have witnessed that will become more clarified, their meaning and purpose known by our exposition. Some of these events have left the world puzzled and worried for many years. We can indeed explain how and why they happened.

This introduction will not be lengthy for we feel the body of the book will tell everything necessary and many words offered here would only be repetitious verbiage.

However we want to point out that just reading the book and even memorizing its sub-divisions will not do the job. One must put them into effect, use them, tabulate and analyze the results for this book to be of the use and benefit which it strives to be.

Fortunately we have reached a point in the understanding and use of your language that we can make ourselves quite clear. As our collaborator here might tell you, however, we do still find it almost impossible to understand your idea of jokes or humor. Other than that we are rather proud of ourselves in learning to use her phrases, idioms, manner of expression well enough to put such writings across. We insist that she use her name as author of these books, which she protests. Our purpose is to give her more self-confidence by seeing her name in print, and indeed these works could not have come forth at all at this time without her sustained and patient collaboration. She has extended many of our ideas as well as found words to phrase them more graphically and even pointed out a few fallacies in our interpretations of personalities and events.

We go at once then into a detailed exposition of our tried and tested methods of interviewing those persons who have had or witnessed psychic phenomena of many varied kinds.

I. Conducting Interviews in Psychic Research Outline

A.   Type of experience:
1.   Out of body
2.   Precognition
3.   Dream sequence
4.   Telepathy
5.   Trance state
6.   Episode of endurance or strength
7.   Voices
8.   Inexplicable coincidence
9.   Inner image or vision
10.   Unexplainable noises
11.   Unexplainable movement of objects
12.   Psychokinesis - mental effect on inanimate objects
13.   Poltergeist effects
14.   Feelings of compulsion or inner directives
15.   Overwhelming emotions for no observable reason
16.   Feelings of being watched or followed
17.   Other psychic experiences

B.   Place of being at time of experience
1.   Home
2.   Strange place
3.   In bed
4.   At work
5.   Awake or sleep
6.   Traveling
7.   Church or place of spiritual worship

8.   Alone or with others

C.   Time elements involved

1.   Day or night

2.   Length of occurrence

3.   Number of times event repeated

4.   Timing of psychic event relative to actual happenings

D.   Person involved

1.   Sex

2.   Age

3.   Temperament

4.   Psychological make-up (to be extended later)

5.   Hereditary proclivities to psychic experience

6.   Education and training

7.   Social status

8.   Home situations

9.   Immediate family, husband or wife and children j. Others living in home

10. Parents: living or dead

11. Children: young, living out of home, or deceased

12. Grandchildren, other young children close to heart

13. Living standard

14. Condition of home Work or business Social status Political involvements Religious activities Community service

15. Moral and ethical viewpoints (as observed)

16. Income or scale of living

17. Attitudes

a.   Responsibilities

b.   Business obligations

c.   Community commitments

        d.   Racial problems

        e.   Religions other than their own

        f.   World political events

        g.   Underdeveloped peoples

E.   Health condition of person experiencing event.

F.   Emotional stress leading up to event

    1.   Involvement with others

    2.   Super strong emotional attachment to another

    3.   Emotional loss recently suffered

    4.   Emotional strain of some coming event

    5.   Exceptional stress leading up to event

    6.   Violent emotion at onslaught of event

    7.   Emotional duress during event

    8.   Relief or release of emotion following event

    9.   General emotional tenor of person involved

G.   Mental tension involved in experience and pre-experience

    1.   Recent worries of intense and personal nature

    2.   Long standing worries or problems of intimate nature

    3.   Seemingly unsolvable problems relating to family

    4.   Strain of financial worries

    5.   Business problems of long standing

    6.   Inability to cope with problems

    7.   Inability to answer own questions

    8.   Mental state at onslaught of experience

    9.   Mental images aroused by experience

    10.   Thoughts of self-preservation during event

    11.   Thoughts of others during event

    12.   Endeavor to understand what was happening

13. Recall of any information concerning similar event

14. Conclusion as to the worst that might befall

15. Thoughts of regret or remorse for things undone

16. Determination to better circumstances

17. Attempts to analyze situation and find answers

18. Mental struggle to gain power and win over situation

19. Tentative decisions

20. Conclusion for action

21. Reflection or summation of probabilities

22. Mental thrust into action

23. Thoughts while acting to combat experience

24. Mental state at conclusive action

25. Afterthoughts.

H. Aspects of the experience not readily visible

1. Time relative to emotional status

2. Occurrence during strong emotional battle

3. Belief in future revelation

4. Concepts of psychic realities

5. Estimation of personal involvement

6. Absolute confidence in self

7. Consideration of elements unfounded in fact

8. Strong support from others

I. Experiences relative to size of personal sphere of action

1. Small enclosed "worlds"

2. Expansive "worlds"

3. Rapid or sudden extension of thought

4. Domination of tradition

5. Exercise of ingenuity

        6.   Creative expansion

        7.   Promise of later events

        8.   Inhibition of former fears

        9.   Problems of revelation

        10.   Inheritance of negative factors

        11.   Traditional taboos

        12.   Overwhelming importance of others opinion

        13.   Development of internal strengths

        14.   Consideration of outgoing tendencies

J.   Hypothesis of current meaning

        1.   Instrumental catharsis

        2.   Absolute individualism

        3.   Important changes in life and action

        4.   Small differences in vital information

        5.   Essential growth attributes

        6.   Impossible ambitions

        7.   Nonsense importunities

        8.   Incredible gaps

        9.   Marvelous attainments

        10.   Personal injunctions contributing to success

        11.   Mastering objectives

K.   Complete analysis of change in character

        1.   Objective episodes

        2.   Release of power

        3.   Containment of aspirations

        4.   Purposive action without articulation

        5.   Constant renewal of belief

L.   Representative concerns of individual

       1.   Reputation

       2.   Social status

       3.   Family reception

       4.   Children's approval

       5.   Peer group approval

M.   Conditions of release

       1.   Absence of purpose

       2.   Change of intention

       3.   Absolute panic

       4.   Absorption of impact

       5.   Consultation with others

       6.   Compact resume of experience

       7.   Solidarity

       8.   Magnification of distress

       9.   System of defense

     10.   Abstinence of judgment

     11.   Control of reaction

     12.   Manifestation of change

N.   Moral attitude in retrospect

       1.   Summation of cause and effect

       2.   Witness of emotion

       3.   Consideration of objective factors

       4.   Self-judgment and condemnation

       5.   Withdrawal from surroundings

       6.   Constancy of loyalties

       7.   Production of anti-thoughts

       8.   Preparation of revelation

O. Rejection of experience

    1. Refusal to face facts

    2. Complete rejection

    3. Half musing wonderment

    4. Acceptance of part

    5. Fear of acceptance

P. Complexities of interpretation

    1. Facts obscured by panic

    2. Emotional impact on memory

    3. Conscientious portrayal of exact factors

    4. Inclination to exaggerate

    5. Concern for effect on others

    6. Attitudes of adjustment

    7. Compromise with facts

    8. Concern for after effects or survival

    9. Adjustment to new extension of thought

    10. Allowances for misinterpretation

    11. Permissive attitude toward event

    12. Solitude and loneliness

    13. Examination of self

    14. Self-aggrandizement

    15. Exploitation

    16. Complete withdrawal

Q. Discovery of new values

    1. Extended viewpoint of reality

    2. Consideration of other realities

    3. Promises of future development

    4. Excitement of self-growth

5. Belief in alternate realities

6. Understanding of extended time/space values

7. Opportunities for deeper study

8. Extraordinary insights

9. Adherence to principals

10. Adjustment to changing views

11. Absolute independence of thought and action

12. Constraint of moral evaluation

13. Exploration of opposing realities

R. Concerns of inner significance

1. Training of insights

2. Consolidation of beliefs

3. Abundance of new ideas

4. Concerns of technical inquiry

5. Purposes of evaluation

6. Consignment of responsibilities

7. Freedoms and duties

8. Supportive measures

9. Explanatory revelations

S. Proper analysis of incident

1. Objective vs. subjective viewpoints

2. Integrity of person experiencing event

3. Knowledge of psychic phenomena

4. Frame of reference

5. Study of details

6. Ability to ascertain facts

7. Experience with allied phenomena

8. Practice in analysis

9.   Compensation for misunderstanding

10.   Consideration of practical application

11.   Desire for benefit

12.   Opinions for analysis

13.   Contrary opinions to fact

14.   Control of emotions

15.   Sanctuary

16.   Modesty of attainment

17.   Proposals for analysis

18.   Perspicacity

19.   Analysis of debate

20.   Contrary to former belief

21.   Person's summary of event

     a.   As it pertains to beliefs

     b.   As it pertains to emotions

II. Events *of UFO* Contacts and Their Occupants Outline

Since giving the foregoing Part I of "Conducting Interviews in Psychic Research", our trusted collaborator has made what we believe to be a very valuable suggestion: Why not extend our presentation with a section dealing directly with UFO studies? Surely from OUR own viewpoint we can offer some very pertinent facts to be considered which otherwise might escape notice or of which you might not recognize now the importance.

Rama same months back observed, "Maybe if they stopped some of the concentrated effort to find some pattern of coherence in the sighting of craft and studied instead the contactees, they could find more rhyme and reason in it all." And still later she observed, "The contactees all seem to 'see' or experience according to their own preconceived ideas of Reality, just as those who have mystical visions and after death experiences see what they almost EXPECT to see. And just as I am having an experience dealing with writing metaphysical subjects and psychic interpretations BECAUSE THAT IS THE WAY MY MIND WORKS!"

Well, our precious collaborator has, what you call, hit the nose right on the button. Now everyone laughs! Oh Rama, please correct the saying. Hit the nail on the head. Good Heavens, child, keep me from such errors!

I am Jamie, extending the outline. Hweig would not make mistakes. He has studied her idiom much too long.

The point I make: Rama has seen the truth, the need to study the UFO event relative to the one witnessing or experiencing it. By our psychic abilities we can make each event tailored to fit the recipient.

But Rama also protests that the Earth psychologists are at the wrong end of the observation to see the actual Reality contained in the seeming experience as we see it from our viewpoint. They see the result; we see the cause.

Before God, this confusion of viewpoints is, we confess, the major reason for the many and mighty confusions we have caused.

Which we regret.

The best hope, Rama says, is to give Earth psychologists a realistic and stable viewpoint, a coherent pattern. We believe by extending our outline for the Earth research of UFO phenomena in general, we can become more easily understood, and more quickly accepted by the scientific milieu whom we have unwittingly offended so long.

Now then:

A.   Type of craft

There are seven basic types of "hardware" craft, with many subtypes, experimental usually, but there are countless more "seen" which are psychic manifestations, or illusions.

1.   Circular, flat with dome

2.   Elongated cylinder, sometimes with very blunt ends

3.   Like wings swept back and touching, looking almost like a doughnut if glimpsed briefly

4.   Like two flat saucers, top one inverted, no dome

5.   Balls or circles of light or flame, floating, whirling, spinning, or rushing

6.   Trapezoid (rare)

7.   Cone shape with truncated bottom (also rare)

These are the basic hardware craft; many minor variations. They travel mainly through a time differential, but some through space also, that is, some part of their journey is through space. They use anti-magnetic forces, not anti-gravity. They can exert such force that gravity is overcome.

Here our Rama has interrupted to ask, "Do you mean you come through a time differential, like the future? You mean the future is going to try to change the past, which to you would be us?"

We are not laughing at her question, but we are not answering. We leave it mysterious, but we want it recorded as it has been said.

Now as for the basic hardware craft, these mentioned are the observable types. We can deliberately maneuver these craft to make one appear to the viewer as a shooting star, or a full moon, or a moonrise, or a will o' the wisp.

Psychically, through hypnosis and hallucination we can make a craft look like anything, and we often do, affecting then, not actually the craft, but the mind of the observer. We do not do this for fun or to tease but for much deeper and more serious reasons, which we shall soon reveal. Craft other than the seven basic types are almost certain to be hallucination.

B. Occupants of the craft

1. Human appearing, passable as Earth human

2. Passable as Earth human but with minor differences such as strange colored eyes

3. Humanoid, looking somewhat human; but with major differences in size, shape, or strange facial structure, or other than five digit hands

4. Humanoid and with non-Earth capabilities and actions, i.e. what you cell weird

5. Approaching humanoid in appearance, but with obviously jerky or mechanical actions, robot-like

6. Definite robots, obviously mechanical constructs

7. Fantastically different in appearance from Earth humans but seemingly alive and intelligent with purposeful action and intent.

Now these are the major REAL occupants! Other than these, occupants seen are mostly deliberately induced hallucinations or psychic manifestations. In another story all of this will be lengthily expounded.

Now that we have given the keys to the recognition of the craft and their possible occupants, we can get back to the contactee.

First he is to be researched exactly as the subjects of Part I, then with the addition of the following:

(We think a straight questionnaire would be most simple here.)

C. Something strange, accompanied by a strong emotion, came into your mind just before the sighting or experience. What was it?

1. Like a warning

2. A message

3. A premonition

4.   An apprehension or dread

5.   A feeling of grief

6.   An expectation

7.   Sudden concern for someone

8.   Vast longing or regret

9.   A sudden joy, or even ecstasy

10. A feeling there is a problem you must solve, or

11. A duty you must perform

12. Or other strong feeling or thought

13. Just before the event you may have noticed a sudden strangeness in the atmosphere:

   a.   A sense of stillness, a vast quiet.

   b.   Rushing air without observable wind.

   c.   A strange overall glow, if at night; or conversely if in day, a strong overall sensation of gathering gloom.

   d.   Feelings of a wave of something passing through self, not as strong as vibrations, just a swaying of the inner self.

   e.   Sudden catching and holding of breathe, or very shallow breathing, almost non-breathing.

   f.   Sensation of being surrounded by pinpoints of flashing light, like so many minute fireflies, but about one tenth the size of real fireflies, with white fire, not yellow.

   g.   Any other strange physical sensation or atmospheric observation.

D.   First glimpse of UFO or occupant:

   1. What strong feeling or emotion (fear, disbelief, curiosity) did you feel?

2.   Was the emotion strengthened or counter-acted as event continued, and in what way?

3.   Was there mental contact of any kind? What?

4.   What recognizable feature existed in this event? Did you see, hear, think, feel, and believe something you had experienced once or more times before? Describe previous encounter with that feature.

E.   As event progressed, did a feeling persist that you had been through this before, or had seen this object or this "person" before, and what was the exact "before" as you remember it?

F.   Did any of the occupants seem somehow like "old friends" to you? Describe fully.

G.   What opportunity have you had for studying psychic phenomena? (Here the opportunities are the vital factor.)

H.   Do you habitually, or sometimes, or never

    1.   Read science fiction?

    2.   See "Space" movies or TV?

    3.   Study psychic or occult literature?

    4.   Peruse UFO literature?

    5.   Contemplate suicide?

    6.   Fear going insane?

    7.   Prophesy doom?

    8.   Expect the end of the world?

    9.   Expect the "Battle of Armageddon"?

    10.   Believe in Satan or Hell?

I.   Have you ever seen, or wanted to see:

    1.   Fairies, gnomes, elves?

    2.   Mythological persons or creatures?

    3   Outer space beings?

THIS IS WHERE IT BEGINS TO MAKE SENSE

J.   Are you currently worried about?

    1.   The future of Mankind?

    2.   The course of Civilization?

3.   Life after Death?

4.   The Reality of God?

K.   Are you looking for aid from?

1.   Divine intervention?

2.   Religious philosophy?

3.   Governmental regulations?

4.   Science, technology, education?

5.   Outer space?

L.   Do you wish with all your heart you could do something to better Earth conditions?

M.   Have you given much constructive thought to ways in which the world could be made better, if only —?

N.   Do you feel you might have an important part to play in the coming events?

O.   If an opportunity arose to do some task, large or small, to make all mankind healthier or happier and the Earth a better place to live, would you sacrifice for it?

P.   Have you a particular idea, thought, writing, information, theory, plan, or any such construct or ability that you would put into effect for such purposes, given the opportunity?

Again Rama points out that those persons having only mental contact with UFO personalities (we prefer not to be called occupants as a class, since some of us are not at present occupying craft) should probably be asked some very special questions. Again, a timely observation. So we prepare a list of important questions to use in interviewing persons, such as herself, who are "hearing alien voices", i.e. receiving telepathic communication from supposedly UFO sources.

Special Questions for Mental Contactees

These questions may seem to repeat some of Part I, but should be asked again in this special context.

Why do you believe these voices or the inner communications are from UFO sources, and why do you believe they have chosen you?

What incident or event or circumstances led up to the hearing of the voices? Did you begin the incident in some manner or was it forced or seemingly impelled on you?

Did you object to the coming of the communication, and how strongly?

What impelled you to bring this matter to my (the interviewer's) attention?

Do you feel chosen or honored or pleased that the voices are there?

Was there any objection voiced against you informing others of these events at any time? Was this objection changed later? Relate trend of this change in detail.

Why were there no conditions made under which you would receive the communication?

What is your final verdict as to (a) the origin of the communicators, and to (b) your receiving it?

Do you feel you are being mind-invaded, mind-dominated, or mind-controlled?

If you could be positive as to the source of this communication and that the reason for it was valid and beneficial, would you cheerfully collaborate with it?

Now as our Rama points out, these questions seem to be for our, the UFO people's benefit. Of course we devised them from our viewpoint; to us these are the vital factors.

So we intersperse 10 more questions from your viewpoint. The revelation in the answers of these questions is more significant then you may see at first glance. It will be summed up in Part III as we give the general outline for analysis and consolidation of data, and then reveal the coherent pattern behind all UFO manifestations. We may say, smugly, you are in for a surprise or two!

What was your major reaction to the first time you were told you were in contact with UFO personalities?

Was there a change in either mental or emotional reaction as the event continued?

What was your ultimate decision mentally and emotionally, or what is your present status?

What value do you feel you have derived personally from this mental contact?

If you had a choice would you cut it off at once?

Are you able to detect in any manner the personality characteristics or traits of your communicator? Do you seem to "just know" what they might be saying or doing which does not seem to come telepathically?

Would you want to meet these persons or person?

Who leads the conversations, opens it, carries the most impetus, or asks the most questions, yourself or the communicator?

Are any observations made by him concerning your personal surroundings or events?

Has he offered constructive advice for your personal welfare or happiness?

III. Analysis and Interpretation of Facts
Researched in Parts 1 and II Outline

Rama's observation that a particular psychic experience or event seems to be relative to who experiences it according to the way that person's mind works is most acute and accurate. And in that observation is the key to many mysteries of the world.

Would a simple peasant of the 12th Century have the same mystic experience that a laboratory scientist of Twentieth Century America would? There must be a responsive chord in the human undergoing the experience or it never would have taken place.

That goes for miraculous visions as well as UFO contacts.

But it is not that simplistic—

The chord may not be developed in the individual at the time of the experience; it may be anticipating something that is to be developed in that person twenty or forty years later! Until that development has taken place, the memory of that event is wiped out of his mind. If we wanted to become poetical we could say it is a flower picked before the seed is planted.

For this reason UFO contacts have been wiped out of the contactee's mind until that person's development, or responsive chord, has been formed.

And that is the danger of hypnotizing contactees and bringing out the facts of an incident before the contactee has the necessary abilities and stamina developed to comfortably accept the facts of the experience.

It is dangerous and CRUEL to expose them to such knowledge before they can handle it.

There seems to be no way of avoiding this in today's practices of hypnosis, so the most humane thing we can do is try to reassure the contactees as best we can and however we can. The same applies to other psychic phenomena or experiences, but seldom with such violent repercussions.

We can only offer knowledge and information here that can be used to alleviate such disasters. We hope, we fervently pray, the information will be seriously studied and USED.

A.   Consolidation and summary of facts concerning person's

    1.   Religious life and beliefs

    2.   Health: physical, mental, emotional or psychological

    3.   Education and study interests

    4.   Style and condition of living

    5.   Personal relationships

    6.   Moral, philosophical, and ethical outlook

    7.   Strength of drive, determination, ambition

    8.   World attitudes

B.   Compact short sketch of incident with all important factors

    1.   Type of event

    2.   Time, place, duration

    3.   Mental and emotional stress

    4.   Changes in thought and feeling as event progressed

    5.   Conclusions or final understanding reached

C..   Relationships of person's Reality constructs to event

    1. Does the event fulfill any great emotional longing in the person's life?

    2.   Does it fulfill any life's ambition?

    3.   Does it make up for any deeply regretted lack educational social status job attainments prestige material possessions

    4.   Does it advance person's ideas, beliefs, or spiritual longings?

    5.   Does it enhance his confidence or belief in Self?

D.   Composition of person's ego gratifications

    1. Does this event make him seem smarter or wiser then before?

2.   Does it allow person to appear at great advantage socially, or elevate him in the esteem of family members?

3. Does it show person off as a wit or brilliant raconteur?

4. Does it redeem person in his own eyes for past failures or mistakes?

E. Exceptional results of incident:

1. Does person become dreamy; retire into self?

2. Does person become violently active in crusades to save the world?

3. Does person go quietly but vigorously about some task that has become almost all-important to him?

4. Can person cope with his new awareness of self and Reality, or does he collapse?

5. Does person become authoritative, dictatorial, demanding of others?

6. Does person become calmer, quietly assured, eagerly alert but composed?

7. Does person take new interest in others, becoming more helpful and concerned for all?

IV. Summary and Revelations Outline

Now in summation:

As given, this is but a brief outline that we intend to extend in great explanatory detail as a book. As given here, any psychologist or trained observer could use it most adequately and wisely to ascertain necessary facts.

However, the analysis and interpretation of these facts need more informative material to be consistently useful, and a great deal more information shall be forthcoming when this outline is expanded into a handbook for those engaged in psychical research.

We did promise to close with some revelations. Here then:

Tracing the Coherent Pattern in UFO Manifestations

A. No contact or sighting is accidental. All has been planned for and long awaited by the UFO personalities who are certainly as excited to be permitted at last to make the contact as the contactee is to see or experience them.

B. All contactees have been carefully researched and "computerized" to determine their best possibilities and capacities for furthering the purposes of the UFO people.

C. All contactees have an experience which is chosen as one in which their preconceived ideas of Reality may be seen manifest. That is why some experiences have spiritual significance to the contactee while we stoutly maintain our activities and capacities are psychic only, not spiritual. The event must be recognizable to the contactee as something he can accept and in some measure "understand" or at least feel most comfortable with. We have not been as successful in the past as we wish, but are striving to do better.

D. All contactees receive information according to their life interests because they have been selected long ago and gently coerced all their lives into studies and activities in which their natural proclivities can blend with the ultimate purpose of the UFO people.

E. Most contactees receive silent information "in their minds" which are probably never articulated but which guide them in their future choices. Free will cannot be tampered with, nor can their minds be permanently controlled, though sometimes- temporary curbs are placed on their run-away emotions or imaginations to help them, or us, overcome a big problem.

F.   Contactees, while chosen many years prior to the contact, May never have had any previous direct or hidden contact with UFO personalities but the largest percentage has, without being in the least aware.

G.   Many contactees have become too fearful to be usable in our work and have allowed other influences to dominate them, which leads to personal disaster, even suicide. No self-dominant person has ever suffered as a casualty.

H.   Contactees who become valuable to us are those who can overcome their various fears and who want to do something beneficial in the world. Each has his or her own capacities, which we utilize to the fullest following the lines of his interests and ambitions. We collaborate in their lives; we do NOT enforce obedience to ours.

I.   As we learn better and better processes of communication we can extend much more scientific and technological information through those who are basically scientists "at heart" even though their academic training is not extensive. We prefer to deal with professional people on the technological problems.

Our collaborator here, whom we lovingly call Rama (Ida), has no scientific background or training whatever, and certainly is no mathematical genius! Therefore we utilize her writing abilities along the lines of her greatest interests - all psychic phenomena.

All of our present contactees, whom we contact daily, are ordinary everyday type of people, those who are not overly prominent in any field, and who live quiet unassuming lives. Rama calls herself "A little old lady in tennis shoes", which is somewhat of a misnomer, for we find she has far keener analytical and deductive abilities and organizational capacities than we had previously ascertained. A surprise to us this time! Her great shyness and lack of self-confidence has indeed "hidden her light under a bushel".

K.   All contactees have one factor in their background. This will knock the tennis shoes off Rama. All have an innate capacity for loving far beyond the normal. All are persons intensely concerned with the welfare and happiness of others.

L.   All contactees have one more factor in common: to a world only now relearning the facts of reincarnation this may seem a dubious statement, but all contactees made a commitment to this collaboration before they were born into life on the planet Earth!

This fact could be verified through the proper use of hypnosis, but the world has forgotten those secrets. With Rama's cooperation, we are going to write books on a host of psychic and allied phenomena. We have already given her tentative outlines for two books, (1) The Development of Telepathic Abilities, and (2) Study of Hypnosis, Its Cause and Effects. Also we have given her titles, or more accurately, subject premises of four more books, (1) Mechanics of Dreams, (2) Symbology of Hallucinations, (3) Validity of Fantasy, and (4) Attributes of Correspondences in Dreams, Hallucinations, and Fantasy. She complains she knows nothing about these, but we tell her that is why we are here, to teach her and to have her help us write these books.

She cannot complain that we intend to let her get lazy!

From the section given here on tracing a coherent pattern of UFO manifestations, a multitude of questions could be derived to further the interviews if desired, but for the present we have been wordy enough.

Rama says she now sees more clearly why the manifestation of UFO incidents (indeed of all psychic phenomena) seems to be experienced according to the way the recipient's mind works, and that this has caused Earth psychologists to believe it could be all fantasizing or from the subconscious of the person experiencing, a conclusion drawn from the fact of reviewing the incident from the viewpoint of effect not cause.

But when Psychic Cause is an unknown, how can interpretation be other than it is?

For this reason we are putting Rama (Ida) to work on the projected books which we know will be of inestimable value in allowing researchers to reason from the basic causes toward the effect and not vice versa.

Thank you,
From Jamie and Hweig
Rama's (Ida's) teachers, friends, and collaborators

P.S. We have given her the name of Rama, which is actually a nice little title rather than a personal name, and use it in all writing because she cringes to see Ida, Ida, Ida all over the pages - a very shy person.

P.P.S. Ida (Rama) speaking: I'm getting over it! With these foreigners listening to my every thought and watching every action, who could remain THAT shy?....

V. Analysis and Summary of Facts
Ascertained in Parts 1 and II Outline

We have given a most comprehensive outline of facts to research for those who have had psychic experiences including UFO manifestations of several kinds.

How then do we categorize and evaluate these facts to reach a useable, functional and understandable conclusion from all this? A complete survey could be evolved here and if done from Earth viewpoint would be invaluable, particularly in analyzing UFO contactees. From the material here to be given, a computer survey can be, and should be drawn.

First, the facts have essentially been categorized by the classifications of the questions themselves. No need to repeat this process, but to extend it into usefulness.

You will find on tallying the responses to these interview questions that the ones who have had the experiences fall into various classifiable niches:

A. The introvert who day dreams, fantasizes, reads literature on psychic events, stays much alone, and is not responsive to group control.

B. The outgoing person who joins all kinds of group activities is controlled by traditional beliefs, borrowed attitudes, and rigid concepts.

C. The intermediate person, sometimes preferring to be alone, not given to rash or hasty decisions, scientifically oriented though perhaps not a cut and dried scientist, able to consider new ideas, a bit adventurous, dedicated to useful purposes, self-disciplined, loyal.

D. The person who is mercurial, changeable, able to adapt to circumstances like a chameleon, usually a little defensive and self-righteous, and lives in a somewhat narrow world, but with very flexible ideas. A will-o'-the-wisp indeed. He does not know himself!

E. The person who elevates himself above the "common herd". He believes he has a mission to save the Earth or mankind. He believes he is endowed by Spiritual forces with special abilities and privileges. He can be paranoid and dangerous in his fanaticism and his single idea approach to life.

F.   The person who has no control in governing himself but must be told most explicitly what to do in any given instance. While not actually retarded, he is immature both emotionally and mentally. He can be used by other forces, malevolent or beneficial, whichever attracts him most seductively.

For our purpose:

These are the main categories of human personalities. There are many sub varieties and of course there can be some, but not a great deal, of overlapping of these.

These are the general categories on which we base our own tests of prospective contactees and workers for us. You will find this evident in the experiences various contactees will report.

Since our interest herein deals with the persons and not the manifestations, we shall proceed with our analysis on that basis.

Now we come to a statement that will give you much thought and perhaps create some argument, but it is a very, very important statement, and after due consideration and study we know you will see the evidence of it:

Persons in each of these classifications are most apt to have specific kinds of psychic experiences for IT IS NOT THEY WHO SEEK THE EXPERIENCE, IT IS THE FORCES OF THE MANIFESTATION WHICH SEEKS THEM. In this they are NOT masters, they are puppets, BUT ONLY TO THE DEGREE THEY ALLOW THEMSELVES TO BE.

The purpose of this is to study the person involved, to show why and how they have a certain experience or certain types of experiences, and to show how they may control or manipulate such experiences at will.

Once the formulae are set down here, it will be possible for any trained psychologist or other well trained and experienced observer to (a) anticipate what kind of psychic experience any known personality is apt to have, or (b) to know from a reported experience what type of person the one who experienced it would probably be.

This gives a method, or repeatable experiment, and a basis for true scientific analysis of such events/persons.

And that is the value of this writing.

We repeat:

A complete survey can and should be devised to facilitate the tabulation and analysis of the survey. The whole evaluation of any person/event can be taken in four or five hours rather than weeks.

To engender interest in and to aid in such a survey, we continue our summation.

In obtaining each of the facts of our interview it is not wisest to ask too direct questions, as other surveys of your world has well known. The survey questions are camouflaged but more than that, they can be melded in such a manner that one pertinent question can lead to a response that will divulge four or more required facts. This, of course, must be done in an inoffensive manner, so that no negative affects arise from a touchy interviewee. All of this is patent.

What is not so easily seen is the total psychological effect on the interviewee, the aftermath. We have learned this ourselves the very hard way! If he or she is left with the feeling of having their most intimate thoughts or secrets invaded, they will be left more antagonistic than cooperative. If they begin to worry later as to "What is going to be done with all this information; who gets it?" as though they might have been disloyal to themselves and others, this too will render them antagonistic; a bad stance.

If they consider the whole interview unnecessary and a time waster when they want to tell their troubles, they will again become impatient and negative.

Therefore, it must be stated clearly in advance that the purpose for the interview is to help them understand and cope with their problems and experience. If they have sought the aid of the one who interviews, so much the better. Also, the help must be given that can be done thoroughly with the final instructions of this treatise.

Secondly, it must be clearly stated that the information derived is to be used by the interviewer for a definite purpose, and in a specific manner, and for the perusal of only specified personages. It is best to have a form of release signed by the one interviewed, a kind of "fee" for the help given. Because of the current tendencies of the world, such a release is a must.

The Procedure then is to tell the one interviewed you will give careful attention to his complete story without any interruptions, unless a little prompting is necessary, and that you will ask fill-in questions and finally he will complete a written survey. Of course all this sounds very trite and ordinary to our trained interviewer. This is written for the sake of training new interviewers, as this is going to become a very necessary and usable process in the near future, the gathering and amalgamation of an inconceivable number of psychic experiences. Many interviewers will need to be trained and ready, and while the training and summation will proceed from one well-established authoritative institution, not yet chosen, the trainees will need a very quick method answerable to scientific requirements. We offer this outline for that training.

When the TIMED experiences of many UFO contactees have reached the moment of revelation, the interviewers should be ready.

The perfect and almost necessary procedure is to tape record the interviewee's story, at least that much, and if they are also willing to have the question and answer and discussion periods tape recorded, that too is most excellent. In this manner, along with the general survey, the whole picture is indelibly recorded. No chance for refutations or denials. Such recording is most necessary for UFO experiences. For other psychic events a less formal study may be given. Stenographic recording may be used also.

We are trying to offer this materiel in its broadest scope, applicable to many types of manifestations that might bear much or little on UFO events. (So many of them are still hidden or obscure, and must remain so for a period of time).

We have not taken into account the many preferences the interviewee may have in the recording of his story. Allowances should be made for individual requirements. This means if he does or does not want his material used in publications, either scientific journals or papers, or more popular books or magazines. Also does he or does he not want it reviewed by various authorities of one kind or another, research groups, scientific analysis, or even military or governmental agencies. The one interviewed must be catered to in this respect in order to gain his best collaboration. It is part of the ethics of the affair, and such a word once given must be scrupulously kept.

It certainly goes without saying that an interviewee's story should never become the topic of social conversation; such is unthinkable!

Catering to such, or other specific requirements of the one interviewed, should impose no hardship whatever on the interviewer. There are many ways to circumvent too stringent restrictions on the gathering, recording, analyzing, or the use of such material.

Fortunately, most persons being interviewed will have asked for help and therefore are most amendable to the interview requirements.

The fill-in questions will comprise two parts: (1) questions aimed to elicit self-responses that will console, calm, or otherwise alleviate the distress of the one interviewed, and (2) questions to complete the needs of any categories not covered in the story. This will require great flexibility on the part of the interviewer, but this comes with much study and practice. No one can read this outline and run right out and start interviewing, unless he has been previously well trained in such procedures for other material. Easy interviews should be attempted in the first stages of study, of mild occurrences and not too seemingly vital events. Sometimes, however, very vital factors are camouflaged under what seems to be quite innocent or naive exteriors. All psychic events should be handled with great discrimination and tact.

The outline itself should be practically memorized, if not in exact detail, at least in category, so that no essential factor is left uncovered.

However, the written survey, which we have not yet devised but will be given later, will at least tabulate any missing fact, though it will not then be given its emotional overtones that verbal response would elicit.

Since each event is unique, and each individual equally unique, fill-in questions that will cover every circumstance are rather difficult to promulgate in advance.

Here we have given the survey material, its meanings and implications. Once these are thoroughly digested, they will help in promulgation of the necessary fill-in questions.

Later, all the foregoing material will be evaluated and extended into one very long handbook. Right now we think it imperative to give these preliminaries, which will prove to be quite useful just as they are to those persons ready and willing and able to use them.

VI. Interviews in Psychic Research Letters Outline

A master psychic among the ETs can call you forth in your semi-corporeal body and you can walk through the solid doors and walls of your house as well as he, or the minions he has sent to fetch you. You cannot walk through the semi- corporeal doors of a craft, however, for you and it are both in the same degree and state of density. You must open and enter doors of a same density place. All this while your wholly physical self waits in its recliner or bed, frozen by hypnosis.

Note on Hypnosis and Mind

PROPER USE OF HYPNOSIS IS THE KEY TO ALL PSYCHIC ADVENTURE.

Do not worry you will be abandoned or misplaced on your adventure wherever it may be. If, for an instant, you "go out of mind" of the Master Psychic, you will wake with a jump and start "back home".

Your "mind" that goes traveling with you is all one mind. It knows a lot more than you do and can take you safely home again in any emergency, or when released by the Master Psychic.

If you were to meet a friend or relative while in this other consciousness state and he tried to touch you, his hand would go right through you to his great consternation. You would be of a different density than his hand. If he tried to photograph you, you would not show up on his film which is in the wholly physical state. This is why many a UFO or even occupant or any other object you thought you photographed does not show up when the film is processed.

No harm can come to you while you are in this state; the only thing to give you distress is your own fear. Strong fear can create the sense of pain. If a craft's occupant passes his hand over your eyes and the pain leaves, he is erasing the fear. You are really confident he has erased the pain is what erases it.

Hypnosis is simply a release of the mind into NON-TIME and that is really the home of the mind; that is where it should be. And from there be free to travel wherever it darned pleases— no space-time limitations whatever.

Some of the processes used by the hypnotist are correct enough. What causes damage is the manner in which the problem to be solved is outlined and the answer requested. For example, instead of telling the person to "go back in time" to such and such an age and report what is happening, the hypnotist should say:

"You are having trouble finding your lost keys. When I count to ten, your mind is now free. It can travel anywhere. There are no space and time barriers. Now it is going to emerge in the exact space and time where you lost your keys. Where are you now? What day is it? What are you doing with your keys? Etcetera.

By this method a mind can find out anything it needs to know from its own experience, past, present, or future. To a mind thus freed there is no limitation of time, no limitation of space, no limitation of knowledge to anything that concerns its own activities. The one vision that is prohibited is the future event of your own death. This would be too unnerving and a source of constant concern so that the mind could not function well thereafter.

One may have a premonition of his own death, or may see a vision or dream of his own funeral. He will not be shown the manner of dying or the date. From factors in the vision he does see (of his own funeral) he may detect whether it is immediate or distant but dates cannot be given.

Hypnosis—Mind Travel—the event is not relived from the present, but lived at exactly the time it occurred. Mind reports the event as it occurs, the one and only time. "Memory" does not go back.

Fantasy: You cannot fantasize something which has never occurred or which is not going to occur in the comparatively near future.

Pictorial telepathy has a language symbology which all use just as we all use "happy" a word symbol. It addition pictorial telepathy can use specific scenes for individual persons acting in a certain way, or factual representations of specific objects or events, etc.

Memory is a "tunnel" between the sub-conscious and the conscious.

Developing Telepathic Abilities Outline

I. Type of person liable to develop good telepathic abilities

Mental set

Religious background

Mature outlook on life

Present emotional states

Current abilities to concentrate

Absolute confidence in self

Willingness to suspend skepticism

Knowledge of psychic phenomena

Belief in beneficial agencies

Freedom from emotional pressures

Ability to relax mind

Time to give to practice

II. Measure of confidence in validity of experience

Belief in aid from unseen sources

Acknowledgement of benefits received psychically

Ascertainment of types of experience- categorizing

Certainty (belief) in results

Denial of self-aggrandizement

Problems of satisfying ego

III. Types of experience relative to telepathy

Hunches

Prognostication

Intuition

"Unheard" voices, warnings

Many results of prayer

Forms of premonition

"Accidental" events

Promises of aid

IV. Emotional involvements in telepathy

Relationships of those involved

Emotional ties of long standing

Classes of experiences

Making most of attempts

Pressures on mental attitude

Terms of maturing relationship

Mutual understanding of those involved

Knowledge of self

Understanding of goals

Acknowledgement of help

Common desire of attainment

Sustained endeavor

Problems solved

Purposes explored

Reasons for attempting telepathy

Problems of evolution of telepathy

Notices of intent

Exercise in coherence

Experiments in custom

Problems of unwilling subject

Attitudes of deplorable nature

Consequence of habits

Expenditure of energies

V. Manner of developing telepathy

Between cross-relatives as twins, brothers, etc.

Between unrelated but allied by interest persons

Between humanity and its animals

Between husband and wife or sweethearts

Between teacher and pupil

Between distant correspondents (this one very important)

Between unknown strangers

VI. Happenings of transmission

Coalition of interests

Expense of operation

Events of alternate choice

Problems of coincidence

Energy reduction and waste

Absolute maintenance

Belief in other events

Cooperation in memory

Experience in dream sequence

Jurisdiction over events

VII. Beginnings in experiences of telepathy

Children and spontaneous experience

Educated trial and error

Development of special abilities

Ties of opposite gender

Motives of special attainment

Increase in potentialities

Exercises to strengthen energy expenditures

Reciprocal exchange

VII. Manner of detecting telepathy

First reception

Factors of receptivity

Analysis of material received

Problems of interpretation

Method of recall

Sensitivity to stimuli of telepathy

Answers to self-questioning

Responses, mode and energy

Belief in receptivity (reception)

Collective experience

Strength and quality of reception

IX. Developing transmission

Power of thought

Clarity of thought

Distinct sensation of sending

Belief in efficacy of sending

Knowledge of telepathy

Power of concentration

Status of belief (faith)

Comprehension of psychic qualities

Progress of value

Conspiracy of intent

Absolute justice!

X. Control of efforts

Comprehension of factors involved

Apprehension of factors involved

Experiments in receptivity and transmission

Careful analysis of results

Manner of selection of topic

Elements of surprise

Problems of comprehension

Latter events correspondence

XI. Structure of Analytical Plan

Problem of issue

Control of event

Analysis of answers to questions

Problems of consultation

Factors of inheritance

Message of hope

Guidance in affairs

Conduct relative to events

Desires beyond possible explanation

Contract of mutual help

Consultations of related issues

Manner of presenting facts

XII. Apprehension of complete control

Belief in self-dependence

Promises of absolute authority

Conduct of permissiveness

Exercise in comprehension of data

Problems relative to existence

Notices of relationship

Designated ending

Complicated structure

Guided release

Objective control and concentration

Elusive elements

Programmed power structure

XIII. Trials of conversational ability

Beginning sentences and phrases

Concentrated effort at structural detail

Problem of analysis

Mechanics of belief

Designated areas of transmission

Limits of thought

Awareness of contact

Problems of analytical character

Circumstances of event

Culmination of enterprise

XIV. Design of achievement

Purpose and direction

Pattern of thought

Constant re-play

Instances of neglect

Models of transposition

Concerted efforts of effect

Program of achievement

Working ends

Satisfaction of design

XV. Constant supervision

Self-discipline

Achievement through negation

Paralysis of intent

Mustering of courage

Problems of self-control

Answers to self-questioning

Instances of self-deceit

Outside influences

Mode of interpretation

XVI. Power to act at will

Strengthening of will

Probable causes of failure

Intent intensified by hope

Attitude toward attainment

Concern for other entities

Knowledge of causes

Attitude toward failure

Marvel at self-attainment

Suggestion of possible power failure

Matters of health

XVII. Excitement of Success

Attainment of aims

Probable rewards

Excess energy releases

Matters of personal concern

Pleasure of achievement

Self-glory

Victory over defeat

Problems of enlightenment

Sustain knowledge

Fulfillment of purpose

XVIII. Attitude toward progress

Belief in efficacy of attainment

Knowledge of self-awareness

Aims of undistorted fact

Need of self-advancement

XIX. Problems of enlightenment

Control of convictions

Absence of interference

Problems of self-aims

S. Attitude towards rewards

Self-effacement

Impatience with results

Probable causes of doubt

Essences of meanings

Program of enlightenment

Excitement of progress

Realization of dreams

Decisions to progress

XX. Decisions of last minute preparations

Finality of achievement

Possibilities of fraud

Contract of obedience

Opportunity at self-effacement

Decisions of ultimate concern

Discovery of inner abilities

Excitement of new adventure

Possibilities of evolved mental state

Measurements of intellectual attainments

XXI. Concern for greater advancement of race

Man's future mental abilities

Spread of abilities

Extraordinary results

Design of evolution

Monitoring of future controls

Belief in evolved behavior

Advancement technologically relative to mind control

Controlling factors in mental advancement

Problems of inter-related areas of mind control

Release of tension and fear

XXII. Summary of purposes

Involvement of self

Attitude towards others

Belief in human race

XXIII. Summary of equipment

Inheritance

Education

Self-analysis

XXIV. Summary of results

For the good of Self

For the good of Man

For the good of EXISTENCE

Ida M. Kannenberg

A pioneer researcher of the UFO enigma, Ida Kannenberg sponsored with Dr. Leo Sprinkle the First Rocky Mountain UFO Conference in 1980 at the University of Wyoming. At the historic conference, she introduced the time travelers that contacted her in 1940.

"Like most UFO abductees or contactees, she [Kannenberg] sees herself as an unobtrusive, unimportant, 'everyday person,'" wrote Dr. Leo Sprinkle. Kannenberg wrote about UFO encounters as she experienced them, information conveyed by the time travelers, and observations about them. She puzzled over composite human nature, humanity as a species, how the species came to its present evolution, and the individual as an existential filament of physical and spiritual worlds. Yet, Kannenberg puzzled in down-to-earth terms and called herself a little old lady in tennis shoes. She extended a steady hand in support of fellow contactees and abductees, and her first book was a manual for UFO experiencers.

A tireless researcher, she wrote seven books about UFO contact, psychic development, ultraterrestrials, extraterrestrials and time travelers. Her books include *UFO Initiation: Ultraterrestrial Time Travelers*; *Project Earth from the ET Perspective: Mind and Species*; *Time Travelers from Atlantis*; *My Brother Is a Hairy Man: The Search for Bigfoot, A Son of Old Atlantis*; *Reconciliation*; and *The Alien Book of Truth.*

Ida Kannenberg was born October 27, 1914 in Iowa. She passed from this life on May 17, 2010.